A VIEW

from the

HEARTLAND

Everyday Life in America

DAVID CHARTRAND

GUILFORD, CONNECTICUT

Portions of this book have been previously published in different form in various newspapers.

Text design: M.A. Dubé

Library of Congress Cataloging-in-Publication Data
Chartrand, David.
    A view from the heartland : everyday life in America / David Chartrand.— 1st ed.
        p. cm.
    ISBN 0-7627-2732-2
    1. Middle West—Description and travel. 2. Middle West—Social life and customs. 3. National characteristics, American. 4. Middle West—Biography. 5. Chartrand, David. 6. Chartrand family. I. Title.

F355.C48 2003
977'.033'092—dc21
[B]   2003056371

Manufactured in the United States of America
First Edition/First Printing

For Mom and Dad,
Steve, Annette, Lucy,
Ed, Art, and Nancy

CONTENTS

ACKNOWLEDGMENTS

This book came to pass mostly because Mary Norris at The Globe Pequot Press believed in it. My writing career came about because Mr. Bishop, my high school English teacher, inspired me to read, because my architecture professor in college urged me to change majors, and because my first copy editor, Ward Harkavy, beat into my head the correct usage of "that" and "which." Deadlines were met because Brian, Cindy, and the other cafe proprietors around Olathe, Kansas, supplied me with bottomless cups of coffee, only some of which I actually paid for. Boundless patience and love were provided by Kathy and Max. I am indebted to all of them for showing me that this is where I belong, that this is what I want to be when I grow up.

YOU CAN SEE BETTER
FROM DOWN HERE

While flying from one coast to the other, I have been known to jab the person next to me—the one nearest the window.

"Look down there!" I say. "That's where I live. The Midwest."

I usually do this somewhere between Kansas City and Denver, although the sky over almost anywhere will do.

The jabbed stranger always flattens his face against the glass and begins to squint downward. He always looks puzzled. And he always says the same thing.

"Where? I don't see a damn thing. Everything looks the same."

While he is squinting, I steal his peanuts.

There is a serious point I wish to make here, though I admit it isn't much of one. Just because you don't see something doesn't mean it's not there. What looks unimpressive or dull to you may strike me as heartwarming and hilarious. Books and movies are like that. So is the view from an airplane. You peer down and see a place to avoid; I see one I cannot bear to leave.

I see home and family and memories. Don't bother asking if they are sad memories or happy ones. From way up here, they all look the same to me.

It goes without saying that the Heartland doesn't look like much from an airplane window. Not that this keeps people from saying it over and over again. "Why would anyone live there?" is the question I get a lot, usually from people who don't live there.

I know how they feel. Having lived few other places, I peer out the window as we pass over New York or Miami or Los Angeles. "Who would live there?" I ask the person next to me, keeping a close eye on my peanuts. Pretty soon the two of us are comparing notes about his homeland and my homeland, both of which, after quite a bit of comparing, begin to look alike. My land is your land. Your land is my land. Before you know it, we are singing that song, just to get it out of our systems.

A view isn't much use without information from the ground. Nothing looks very interesting from 30,000 feet until the pilot points out what you are looking at and why you should bother looking at it. Then you have to ask yourself what you think you are looking at, and soon the other passengers begin asking the flight attendant what she thinks you are looking at. Before you know it, all hell breaks loose.

It would be more helpful if the pilot were to announce:

"Down there, just beyond the right wingtip, is a three-story Dutch frame house belonging to Arthur and Chris Chartrand of Kansas who raised three daughters and four bouncing boys, two of whom are still bouncing. See it over there? The one with the wood shingles on both sides? In 1969 the house was accidentally set ablaze while being painted by one of the Chartrand sons, who wishes not to be identified. His name is available upon request. He is David Chartrand and he is asleep in Seat 4-C on this flight, having sedated himself with Dramamine due to a lifelong case of chronic motion sickness. If you look closely, you'll notice that there are people like the Chartrands all over the Heartland due to the fact that there are people like them all over America—people who believe that families are more important than careers, that love is more important than money, that poking fun at local politicians is more fun than electing them, and that you have to work hard every single day at everything you do because it all can be taken from you in an instant. This has been your pilot speaking. Relax and enjoy the flight."

The passengers would nod approvingly. (Adverbs are not my friends. Is it possible to nod disapprovingly?) They would finally understand what they were looking at. It would be clear to them why someone would want to remain connected to such a dull and uninteresting place. They would have reliable information based on life down below rather than the dim view from above.

"Now we see it," everyone would say. "What a good view we have."

<hr />

The following pages represent my view from the Heartland, and the Heartland from my view. If memory serves me right, everything happened exactly as I have written it here. I have omitted plenty, which I attribute to a bad memory, which in turn I attribute to watching too much television with my brothers and sisters when I should have been reading books.

It isn't so important how much we remember, however. What matters is how much we *learn* from what we remember. It is a paradox of human perception that we see events more clearly the farther back we stand. The farther back I stand, the more I can see that my life was shaped by friends and family who forgave me for my mistakes, who helped me see that happiness is found in being connected to something bigger than self or career or money.

You can learn this anywhere, but I learned it growing up in the Heartland. Living in Middle America is like sitting at center court. It is the 50-yard line. Box seats. From here you witness all of America and everything American. It is a land of contradiction and contrasts, an unpredictable place that can revivify your spirits and drive you to your knees. It batters you with good times and hard times, not to mention winters that numb your feet and summers that blister them. Eventually it forces you to see the difference between the things that keep you happy and the things that just keep you busy.

If you've never seen it from the ground, the view from the Heartland may surprise you. It may seem strangely familiar, as though you've seen it before. Take a good look. If you squint, it might even look like home. Wherever that is.

Okay, you can quit looking now and pull your seat and tray table to their full and upright positions. The plane is making its final descent into the Heartland.

By the way, someone just stole your peanuts.

⸎⤬⸎

ONE

EVERYDAY PEOPLE

Flying Away

I am driving my seventy-nine-year-old parents to the Kansas City airport. They are trying to relax. So am I.

"You'll do fine," I tell them. "Airlines do this every day. You're going to have a great time."

It's been a long time since my folks have been on a plane, even longer since they have been out of the Heartland. Today they are flying to Boston for a New England vacation with my brother.

Eating fresh lobster and seeing the ocean, however, are not on my mother's mind right now.

"I need to keep my cane," Mom says from the backseat for the third or fourth time. "They'll let me keep my cane on the plane, won't they?"

Yes, they will, Mom. It'll be fine. You'll see.

I am telling her this, but what I am thinking is, *Please, please, dear God, let this go well. Please let there be no long lines at the airport. Let there be a place to park so I don't have to leave these two people all alone at the gate.*

1

We pull up to the Midwest Express terminal. Drat. There are long lines. There are crowds. There is no place to park.

"Lot of people traveling today, huh?" Dad says. He is acting like this is fine with him, but I can tell it isn't. "Help your mother," he says. "I'll be fine."

"I'm sure glad you know about airports," Mom says, hugging my arm as I help her out of the backseat. "How'd you get to be so smart?"

I got it from you, Mom. She thinks this is very funny.

I glance across the top of the Camry. My eyes notice Dad stepping out of the passenger's side. Then I see him fall straight down. An audible gasp from a young woman sitting on a nearby bench rearranging the contents of her purse.

Dad caught his foot on the curb. His arms are bleeding. He is looking up at me. It's probably the way I looked up at him that time when I was seven and I fell at the swimming pool after he had warned me to walk.

"I'll be okay," he says. "I bleed easily. It's all that heart medicine."

Please, God, let everything be fine.

I drag their bags inside. The check-in line is even longer now. I wish I could quiet the crowd for a minute and get everyone's attention. I wish I could announce that these are my parents and that everyone should be nice to them.

I would tell everyone that Arthur and Christianne Chartrand have not traveled very much because they never had a lot of money, and they didn't have money because they had seven kids. Travel and money weren't important because we spent our whole lives in the Heartland. I would explain that summer vacations usually consisted of a road trip to my aunt's house in Garden City, Kansas. Five hours in a blue Ford station wagon full of kids and swimsuits. If anyone in this noisy terminal was still listening, I would tell them how we laughed and laughed the time Dad hit a skunk on I–70 and the station wagon stank so bad we had to hold our noses the rest of the way home.

If I could just explain all this, then everyone would understand how important these two people are to me. But there is no time.

We finally get our turn at the check-in counter. The ticket agent is an attractive woman in her forties. Her badge says LYNETTE. She has fine friendly lines around her mouth. I can tell she knows how to soothe anxious elderly travelers. I can tell she knows how to soothe the children of anxious elderly travelers.

"This is my son," my mom announces as Lynette taps on the keyboard. "He's a writer."

Lynette smiles back and makes warm eye contact. "You must be proud of him." Mom beams. Thank you, thank you, Midwest Express, for having Lynette on duty today.

Getting through security comes off with only thirty or forty hitches. Mom trips the alarms repeatedly with her rosary beads and pillboxes. Dad is asked to remove his shoes. This takes a while when you are seventy-nine with bad knees.

Now a flight attendant is offering an elbow to mom. "You can walk down the jetway with me if you'd like," she says. "You're in 4-D and 4-C." Mom is relaxed now. She releases my arm and takes this new one.

"We'll be fine," Dad says. "Everyone in this airport knows your mom now, so she's happy. Thanks for everything."

Slowly, the three of them vanish down the jetway.

<hr/>

After a minute or so, I turn away. My eyes catch the glance of a sixtyish woman with short-cropped hair, wearing a denim vest and a denim skirt. I wonder if she notices how hard it is for me to swallow right now.

"Your parents?" she asks.

I nod. She is smiling the way people do when they see

things from a distance, like love and pain, and they understand without anyone having to explain.

"We never traveled much," I say. "They liked staying home, with us kids."

The denim lady smiles. "I'm sure they'll be fine."

I say nothing. Another slow, dry swallow. The jetway door closes.

"Yeah. They'll be fine."

Whither the Doves

There are stories that Christianne Chartrand loved to tell over and over again about her children. One was about the day she took her firstborn, Steve, to his first day of kindergarten at Christ the King Catholic School.

"I cried and cried," she said at family dinners, to anyone who was paying attention. "I was so worried that he might be scared of the nuns or that the other kids would be mean to him." All of us would groan.

We know, Mom, we know. We've heard this one a million times.

She tuned us out. "One of the nuns, I think it was Sister Anna Marie." She called out to Arthur, her husband, who was in the next room scraping dishes, "Honey, what was the name of that nun who was Steve's kinder-garten teacher? Honey?" Arthur had tuned her out. He had heard the story a million times, too.

"Oh, your father never listens to me," Chris said. "Anyway, Sister WhateverHerNameWas. She took his hand and told me I just needed to walk away."

"She said if I just walked away and let him go, he'd be fine. Boy, she was right. Soon as he saw the other kids on the playground, man, he was gone."

Then Mom tilted her head to one side and brought her hands up to her breast, palms up. It was her *what-can-you-do-about-it* gesture.

"He didn't even wave good-bye," she said.

My mother told this story as though it were a parable whose lesson was self-evident. There was no sadness in her voice.

Some voice is always telling us to let go. Believing that voice is one thing; obeying it is another.

⸺✕⸺

In "Bark," a *New Yorker* short story by British author Julian Barnes, a friend asks Jean-Etienne Delacour why, at the age of sixty-one, he had decided to pursue new adventures and loves. Delacour responds that he did not change his life. Life had changed him, and he was powerless to stop it. Consider he says, the man who raises rabbits or bees or doves. If the rabbits flee their warren or the doves bolt their cages, they belong to whosoever may find them. Rabbits have feet to run; bees and doves have wings to fly.

"I mean," Delacour says, "that we make such certainties as we can. But who can foresee when the bees might swarm? Who can foresee whither the dove might fly, or when the rabbit might tire of its warren?

"Who can foresee whither the dove might fly?" he asks again.

My Father's Ladder

There are many types of dads because there are many types of men.

There are men like Fred MacMurray and Jimmy Stewart who come from the broad Rotarian mind of Hollywood, where fathers are always sagacious, unflappable, and protective. But there also are men like Harry "Rabbit" Angstrom and Willy Loman who come from the minds of men like John Updike and Arthur Miller. These are men who remind us that it's hard to be sensible and secure when you feel distracted and purposeless.

There are men who enjoy big families, dinner table commotion, and backyard clutter, and those who require peace and quiet. There are fathers who are good at fixing and mending because their fathers were good at it. Others choose to leave the fixing and mending to others. Fatherhood fits some like a custom-tailored new suit, while others tug and chafe at the yoke of domestic responsibility like an unbroken draft horse.

Boys learn about being fathers by watching. They watch their fathers and they watch other men. This is why there are many types of little boys, which, in turn, is why there are many types of men. Then the men have boys of their own and it starts all over again.

⚛

My father, Arthur Chartrand, was the president of a small Midwest neighborhood bank. He was the kindest, friendliest, most helpful banker there ever was.

Anyone could see that my father enjoyed being a banker. But what he really liked was coming home and getting up on his ladder.

Dad was always on that ladder. That's why I always looked up to him. No one seemed more comfortable dragging a ladder around the house than my pop.

The ladder got him where he needed to go. It got him up in the air, which is where all the broken stuff is on a house. Shingles to be replaced; windowsills to be scraped and puttied; bird poop to be removed from awnings. He was always up there, cleaning and taking care of whatever the ladder could reach. It took a lot of time, but nothing else was more important.

"When you have a house," he would say between pulls on his pipe, "you need to take care of it. Take care of things and they'll last a long time."

If that ladder could listen, and I knew how to talk to ladders, I'd have a lot to say to it. I would thank it for helping Arthur take care of the house. I would point out that Dad was right, too. The house lasted a very long time.

Oh, I'd remind that ladder about the time it lost its footing and the two of them, ladder and banker, went crashing to the ground. Arthur came home with his arm in a cast and a steel pin in his elbow. The pin left him with a permanent crook in his arm, but it didn't keep him off the ladder. It just made him more careful.

Arthur taught his four sons about ladders, too. He had Steve, David, Eddy, and Art Junior up in the air every summer, scraping and painting. The house was wood shingle from top to bottom and side to side. We'd scrape and paint, and scrape some more. Then we'd drag the ladder a few feet and do it again. It would take two summers to scrape and paint the whole house. By the third, it was time to start again.

Sometimes my brothers and I would tire of standing on

ladders in the Midwest summer sun, scraping and painting. We didn't want to know about fixing houses or making things last a long time. We had other plans. We wanted to go swimming or play Home Run Derby with the plastic bats.

Dad would let us quit, but he never quit. After supper we would hear that ladder being dragged again from one side of the house to the other. Some summer evenings we'd hear it until well after dark.

I have a house of my own now and I own two ladders. I only use one of them. I keep the other one around to remind me of my father. When I hear myself whining about how much work it is to own a house and how much time it takes to fix and mend things, I hear him dragging his ladder. Then I get to work. I figure I have nothing more important to do.

Letting Go

The New England vacation turned out fine for Arthur and Chris. I should have known.

My parents had survived things much worse than a congested airport. They were midwesterners. They knew to expect the unexpected every day.

I call them Everyday People—not because their lives are common or ordinary but because they handle the common, everyday vicissitudes of life with an indomitable spirit. They are connected to something stronger than themselves, something that helps them let go of the things they cannot control.

The word that best describes such people is *resilient*. You find resilient people anywhere you find struggle and hard work, wherever life's most predictable feature is its unpredictability. Midwesterners have no monopoly on resilience. They simply possess it in deep, boundless abundance.

The Heartland is a place of conflict, contrast, and incompatibility. BMWs collide with pickup trucks, deer crash into minivans, winter slams into summer, and tornadoes slam into sleeping neighborhoods. Prosperous suburbs encroach upon decaying farm towns. The privileged live amid the uneducated. Fast lanes merge into slow lanes. Family farms share fence lines with meth labs. In such a place life is capable of turning tragic every day.

Resilient people are not exempt from tragedy; they are simply not vanquished by it. University of Pennsylvania professors Karen Reivich and Andrew Shatte have written that resilient people are neither pessimists nor optimists. They are "accurate thinkers" who are "realistically optimistic."

Such people understand that there are no guarantees.

"Realistic optimism does not assume that good things will happen automatically," Reivich and Shatte say. "It is the belief that good things may happen and are worth pursuing but that effort, problem solving and planning are necessary to bring them about."

Resilient people choose to let go of the things they cannot control and remain connected to the institutions that give their lives meaning. For Arthur and Chris, those were family and faith. They had learned long ago that money and good health were temporary but God and family were forever.

Everyday People believe that God and family bring joy into your life, forgive you your trespasses, and give you the courage to let go of the things that aren't important. Most of all, God and family will be there when bad things happen to good people, to rescue and heal them.

The Tyranny of the Urgent

Everyone called him Fast Eddy. Part of it had to do with his fleetness of foot on the soccer field. The rest was a snickering reference to his facility with women. Edward Chartrand was a smooth, handsome stud. None of that matters now.

In May 1979 he was living at home with Arthur and Chris Chartrand, his parents. Our parents. He'd just graduated from college and had begun work as an examiner for the Federal Reserve Bank. Fast Eddy was the first, and only, of Arthur's children to follow him into the banking business.

On Friday evening, May 18, Eddy came home and changed clothes for a date with his girlfriend, Lorie. He probably hollered a good-bye or two on his way out the door. If anyone heard him, it was the last time any of us would ever hear him.

Very late that night, he returned home and undressed for bed. Arthur and Chris were asleep, as was his younger brother, Art Junior, a pre-law student at Kansas State home for the weekend. Sometime after stripping to his underwear, Eddy blacked out and never woke up. He collapsed to the floor in the upstairs hallway, next to the family medicine closet. Maybe his head had been aching and he'd gone looking for an aspirin. Maybe he was having trouble breathing and was trying to call out.

By Sunday afternoon, May 20, Fast Eddy was dead. He was twenty-two years old. Perfect health and perfect spirits. The doctors found no certain cause of death, though there was conjecture later about a sudden cardiac arrhythmia. No one was sure.

None of Fast Eddy's three brothers and three sisters got to give him a final hug. The only one who came close was Art Junior. He said he heard the thump in the night, followed the sound upstairs, and came across Eddy sprawled on the hallway floor. He got to squeeze Ed's warm body one last time as he tried in vain that night to shake life back into the lifeless.

Dad called me long distance with the news. I was a hotshot government reporter for an out-of-state daily newspaper. It wasn't a long drive from my family's home, the home where I grew up. But I rarely visited or called. I hadn't been home for months.

I couldn't help it, could I? I was working on my future. I had been interviewing at newspapers in the Northwest, where my girlfriend lived. I had been busy at work, running here and running there.

All day Saturday and into the night, the Chartrands took turns holding vigil over Ed's body in the St. Joseph Medical Center intensive care unit. My shift was midnight to 2:00 A.M., which wasn't a good thing. I have rarely been able to stay awake past midnight. To this day I can barely drag myself to Christmas Eve Midnight Mass, and I'm the choir director. In the ICU that night, I worried that someone would walk in and notice that I had failed my watch, pointless as it seemed with Ed's vital organs tethered to a menagerie of tubes and monitors. What kept me awake were my shame and the creepy, whissing sounds made by the pumps and monitors whose plastic tentacles sprawled across my brother's chest and face.

Around 2:00 A.M. Dad arrived for the changing of the guard. "David, you better get some sleep," he said. One of Mom's black rosaries dangled from his fingers.

I stood to offer my chair. Dad ignored it and walked to the bedside, near Eddy's head. I stood at his left.

Dad said we should keep talking, just in case some part of Ed's subconscious spirit could hear our voices. Just in case. Then he awkwardly reached down with his left hand and clasped my right, as though he might fall.

"Your mother and I have always been so fortunate . . . ," he said, still squeezing. I thought he was going to say something else. Instead, he brought his right hand to his mouth and clenched it tightly, as though he was about to gag.

My father was fifty-five years old on this night and I was twenty-five. It was the first time I had seen him cry.

Then Dad knelt by the bed. He said I could go now. Stepping into the hallway, I turned back to pull the door softly to the latch position.

As I did, I could hear Dad talking out loud, begging Eddy to wake up.

I think about Fast Eddy whenever I read stories in the newspaper about young people dying suddenly. It happens every day in the Heartland, as it does across America. Car accidents, farm accidents, tornadoes, floods, shootings, suicides, sudden cardiac arrhythmia. I see their names in the paper every day. I don't know their families, nor do I suspect they have grieved any less, or any more, than have I.

I only wonder if they feel the way I did in 1979, the way I still feel: sorry. I feel sorry because I never had the time, or took it, to tell my brother how much he meant to me. Sorry because God snatched him away before I looked him in the face and told him how miserable we'd be if he ever left without saying good-bye.

That's the price you pay for run, run, run. It's the tyranny of the urgent. Always enough time to meet pressing deadlines, but never enough for the important things that have no deadlines. There is never enough time to tell people how much you need them, to let them know how miserable you'd be if they left you in the night without a final hug or farewell.

Perfections

By 1958, Christianne Chartrand's magnolia tree was the talk of the neighborhood. She and Arthur had planted it eight years earlier, right after they moved into the tiny, two-bedroom wood frame in the heart of the Heartland.

Passersby were surprised to see a magnolia tree, surprised that it could withstand the irritable Midwest with its brutal winters and granite-hard clay. Everyone assumed that such a magnificent flowering tree only grew in the Deep South, someplace with even rainfall and well-drained soil. Everyone said that Chris must be very good at making things grow.

They were right about Chris but not about magnolia trees. They were thinking of the grandiflora, the magnolia of southern plantations and picture postcards. Hardy magnolia cultivars, however, had evolved in the Midwest and adapted to its unpredictable climate and impenetrable clay. So had countless hybrids of flowering redbuds, dogwoods, hollies, crabs, hawthorns, peonies, rhododendrons, and viburnums. All of these developed deep roots that sustained them through the scorching and freezing on the earth's surface. Surprisingly beautiful things persevered in the Heartland, along with the resilient Americans who had immigrated and adapted.

Each spring Chris prayed that the first frost would hold off until after the magnolia had bloomed. With any luck that would be after Easter, when she arranged her children, smallest to tallest, in front of the tree. Chris stood back and coaxed the children into stair-step position while Arthur tripped the shutter on the Brownie Starflex (one shutter speed, retail: $10).

Each spring another picture of the magnolia and the children was added to the family photo albums. Chris had as many albums as she had children, and as many snapshots as she had plants and trees. Hers were not the flimsy "scrapbooks" with clear-plastic page sleeves that she would be forced to use thirty years later. Chris bought sturdy photo albums with thick, durable pages that never pulled away from the metal spindles, the ones with removable caps that made it easy to add more pages. Photos were mounted on the page in straight, parallel lines, each held in place with black, triangular adhesive corner holders. Chris's photo albums were built to last for a lifetime.

It made Chris feel good when friends noticed her trees and her scrapbooks and her children. It made her feel good to know there were things she was good at. In gardening and raising a family and making photo albums, she had found her métier. She was good at creating durable, resilient things that lasted a lifetime.

She worked hard at all these things because they gave meaning to her life. Christianne and Arthur were the careful, hardworking Americans who came home from World War II to build perfect communities and raise perfect families with perfect yards and gardens. They believed that if you took care of the things that are yours—loving, meticulous, unrelenting care—then you would have them for a long time. They would grow and bloom and others would marvel at their beauty.

Fifty years later the little wood-frame house is still standing, but the magnolia tree is not. The next owner must have cut it down. Or maybe it was slain by summer drought or winter ice. Over the years Chris learned that some things—including plants and children—don't live forever. There's nothing you can do about it. Life is not always perfect.

Arthur and Chris are in their eighties now, and once again they have moved into a small wood-frame house. Chris is still good at taking care of plants and small children. Her photo albums remain in perfect condition.

Last spring she and Arthur planted a sapling pear tree in their new front yard. Chris saw to it that the trunk was staked ruler-straight and that the hard clay dirt was mulched with healthy, organic compost. She says she wants the tree to last a lifetime. Those who know her have no doubt that it will.

Turning Points

After Fast Eddy died, life was one lousy break after another.

It was as though God had decided to make corrections. He had given Arthur and Christianne too many good times and not enough bad ones. They were midwesterners. Life wasn't supposed to be this easy.

My parents were still adjusting to one less chair at the dinner table when another Heartland family decided to make its own adjustments. I will refer to them as the Bucks Family.

The Bucks were a prominent banking dynasty that controlled several bank holding companies in the postwar Heartland suburbs. Big Daddy Bucks hired young Arthur Chartrand to work in the loan department of one of the Bucks Family banks; a long friendship ensued. Daddy Bucks sometimes dropped fruit baskets at Arthur and Chris's house on Christmas or attended the baptism of one of their seven children.

By the mid-1960s, Arthur was promoted to president of a Bucks branch bank. His office was not upstairs with artwork and a view. Arthur wanted his desk in the lobby, where customers could see the president standing watch over the bank or watching over his children who loved to toddle around the lobby and beg Tootsie Rolls off the cashiers. This

20

made the customers feel good about their bank and their money because they felt good about Art Chartrand.

One day in the late 1970s, Daddy Bucks retired and handed the reins of the Bucks banking empire over to his children.

The Baby Bucks, unlike their father, were not into old-fashioned Midwest community banking, where the board of directors counted progress by the number of new checking accounts. They weren't into fruit baskets. The Baby Bucks, like the other bright young things in the industry, weren't interested in old-fashioned business. They were interested in "financial services." They were tired of the shallow end of the banking pool. They wanted to dip their wingtips into the deep end where you could dive for really big bucks.

By the 1980s banking's future was big commercial accounts, leveraged investments, and bank presidents who ran in the fast lane. Banking's past was passbook savings accounts, small retail accounts, and presidents who stayed in the lobby to greet customers. Arthur was the Spirit of Banking Past, and the Baby Bucks had little use for him. They also had little use for the fine points of interpersonal communication. Arthur came to work one day and found a letter on his desk.

This letter was not a commendation for his many years of service. It explained that his desk was being given to some Brave New Young Buck. It said Arthur could still hang around the lobby and greet customers if he wanted to, but that he should stay out of the way.

Arthur did not want to be in the way, so he said good-bye to the tellers and clerks who had worked for him for years and years, and then cleaned out his desk. The Bucks did not give him a retirement party or a gold watch, but instead gave him a severance package so stingy it would have taken Scrooge's breath away.

The rest is history. The banking business in the 1980s and early 1990s got everything it deserved. American consumers, however, did not. The people who own your neighborhood bank nowadays are not from your neighborhood, and the president is never in the lobby greeting customers. If it's personal attention you want, try the hardware store. Come to think of it, most hardware stores aren't locally owned anymore, either.

I drive past what is left of my father's former bank now and then, but only if I have to. The building brandishes a menacingly abstract logo that belongs to the multinational financial services conglomerate that bought out the bank that was owned by the Bucks who wrote the letter that was left on the desk that belonged to Arthur Chartrand, who came home one day and told his family that he loved them very much but that he didn't love banking so much anymore.

Staying Home

None of us knew it at the time, but Fast Eddy's death and my father's ignominious dislodgment from the bank were only the beginning of the indignities that God and the Midwest are always asking families to endure. In between tree-shattering winters and brick-blistering summers, there were financial nightmares, divorces, emotional breakdowns, and more tragedies.

Relief was provided by the ritual rhythms that sustain all families—holidays, yard work, weddings, babies, graduations, raucous arguments, prayer, and marathon after-dinner games of Pictionary where you laugh so hard you fall on the floor and grab your sides. Though mistakes are made and unfair things happen, never underestimate the healing, forgiving power of family. No matter how many dishes you break, someone still invites you over for Thanksgiving dinner.

As for me, I managed a few inspired moves. I married a hometown doctor's daughter who took over her father's practice, which meant that at least one of us had long-term employment prospects. I rented an office and began working for myself; then I rented space to Dad so he could work for himself. Neither of us knew where the money would come from. My father and I were to discover that we were capable of more than either of us thought possible.

The course of our lives is always being altered by some random calamity or another. After Eddy died and Arthur lost his job, the Chartrands chose to let go of the future. Nothing else seemed important or interesting other than huddling together as a family, at home in the Heartland.

So that's what we did. We let the bees swarm and the doves fly. Where they might land we hadn't a clue. But we were in no hurry to find out. We had nothing else planned.

TWO

EVERYDAY VOICES

To the Heartland, Wherever It Is

I would tell you where the Heartland is, but I don't really know. Neither does anyone else.

A *New York Times Magazine* article about the corporate accounting scandals of 2002 claimed that WorldCom (Clinton, Mississippi) and Enron (Houston) were "Heartland" companies. Tom Brokaw says he grew up in the Heartland (South Dakota).

You could ask people in the Midwest. Midwesterners say they live in the Heartland, but they're not sure where the Midwest is, either.

Or you might ask James Shortridge. A geography professor at the University of Kansas, Shortridge had long been curious about how the Midwest got its name and its reputation. His *The Middle West: Its Meaning in American Culture* (1989, University of Kansas Press) is as close as you'll ever come to a book that makes geography entertaining.

The earliest known reference to the term *Middle West*, Shortridge said, is found in 1827 article about religious unrest in Tennessee. Tennessee probably seemed like the middle of America to someone who was there in 1827.

As America moved west, so did its middle. By the 1880s, Shortridge said, many writers decided the Middle West was Kansas and Nebraska. As you might expect, Kansans and Nebraskans agreed with this idea, but others did not. The more states that joined the Union, the more difficult it was to decide which ones were in the Midwest and which were not.

By 1912, Shortridge continued, there had emerged a precarious consensus that the Middle West was an unofficial roster of about twelve states west of the Mississippi River, give or take a state or two. Nearly everyone agreed with this new definition, except for those who violently disagreed and who felt that the Midwest was definitely east of the Mississippi River.

This confusion about the Midwest continued to vex writers and cultural historians through much of the twentieth century. Eventually they compromised and agreed to forget the whole thing. All that was clear was that every American had his or her own idea about where the Midwest was located.

To demonstrate this, Shortridge sent a survey in 1980 to American college students across the country. The students were given maps and pencils. They were instructed to lay the map on a flat, dry surface and then circle the states that they thought were in the Midwest.

This survey produced two remarkable results. The first was that Shortridge actually got 2,700 college students to take this quiz and mail it back to him. The other significant discovery was that, for most Americans, the Midwest is a figment of their imagination. It is a cultural mirage whose appearance depends on whom you ask and where they are standing when you ask them.

Students from Kansas, Nebraska, Iowa, and the Dakotas tended to draw the Midwest as a tight group of states centered on, well, Kansas, Nebraska, Iowa, and the Dakotas. Students from the Northeast and Southeast weren't sure, but they tended to draw the Midwest as an immense region stretching from the Ohio River to California. A few students from Washington—the state—said they were part of the Midwest.

Students from Ohio, Indiana, and Michigan said the center of the Heartland was well to their west; many Ohioans didn't see themselves as midwesterners at all.

Ohio? Not part of the Midwest?

Shortridge had his own theory about this identity crisis. Midwesterners aren't sure about their borders and boundaries because they frankly don't give it that much thought. Midwesterners don't bray about the Midwest the way New Yorkers do about the Northeast or Californians do about the West. Heartlanders could care less about regional pride.

This, said the professor, probably stems from a "lack of a historical core" for midwestern culture.

"Most major American regions have obvious roots," he wrote. "New England owes much of its temperament today to its puritan heritage; the Southwest, to its Spanish-Catholic and Indian traditions; and the South, to its ruralism and period of independence. The Middle West is more complex. Its early settlers came from Yankee, Middle Atlantic and Southern cultural traditions on the eastern seaboard as well as from Germany, Scandinavia, Ireland and Eastern Europe.

"The more one thinks about the Middle West," Shortridge concluded, "the more muddled the regional identity becomes."

In other words the Heartland is what you get when you reach into a melting pot, pull out a patchwork, and throw it at a hodgepodge.

As far as midwesterners are concerned, it doesn't matter where you live. It only matters where you stand and what you believe. No matter who you are or where you come from, you are welcome to call the Heartland home. Or you are welcome to visit. Just don't ask us for directions.

Harmony is Overrated

By now you might suspect that if Heartlanders don't agree on where they are, they probably don't agree on who they are, either. You would be right.

Midwesterners take great pride in their contentiousness. No one ever had much fun being agreeable all the time. It is much more entertaining to live in a place that celebrates a heritage of diversity and rambunctiousness.

On the second weekend of every September, my Heartland hometown stages a morning-long community parade. Its purpose is to honor our rugged eighteenth-century pioneer ancestors who trekked here from the East across the Oregon Trail and, having missed the turnoff for Oregon, decided to settle in the Midwest. They didn't know it was the Midwest; to them, it was simply an unbelievably hot place in the middle of nowhere.

The annual "Old Settlers Parade" in my hometown is cultural entertainment for the whole family. Thousands of grownups and kids squat under the canopy of maples and elms along Chestnut Street on what is usually the last hot and humid day of the year. Everyone roots or jeers with gusto for the passing procession of historically accurate Toyota 4Runner SUVs pulling flatbed floats upon which are tributes to the cherished traditions of the Midwest. My favorites are the teams of Belgian draft horses hitched to brightly festooned covered wagons, riding upon which are authentically costumed citizens waving huge vinyl banners that read, VOTE NO ON SCHOOL BONDS!! and GILMAN IS A JERK! VOTE WITTENCRAST!! and CITIZENS BANK—TRY OUR NEW ATMS!! It is the best-attended community event of the year.

⁂

From the beginning, the idea of a "Midwest" was on shaky grounds. It was an ambiguous term that could mean different things to different people. As language it was imprecise and often misleading. For these reasons it became wildly popular among American journalists.

Shortridge, the geography prof, noted that writers have long labored to capture the American spirit and then sell it to publications that specialize in portraying the American spirit. *Reader's Digest* comes to mind. In the Midwest writers found the mother lode of American images. What began as a geographic descriptor gradually evolved into a cultural symbol for wholesomeness, morality, and independence.

The Midwest was no longer a place; it was a way of life.

"The Middle West," Shortridge wrote in his book, "had become the standard by which to judge the rest of the nation . . . it came to symbolize the nation and to be seen as the most American part of America." He quoted one writer, John Gunter, as calling the Midwest "America uncontaminated."

(How *Middle West* got abbreviated to *Midwest* or who nicknamed it the *Heartland*, Shortridge could not say. It may have been some copy editor at *Reader's Digest*.)

Never mind that these were sentimental generalizations that could apply to nearly every region in America, both then and now. When we journalists grab hold of a perfectly sentimental generalization, we never let go. Never mind that the symbolism and the sentiment, as with the geographic location, shifted from place to place like the Kansas wind. The Midwest as metaphor for America was here to stay.

Mixed metaphors and gaudy symbolism don't bother midwesterners. Hell, look at our parades. We welcome all kitsch and kin. To some the Heartland represents fierce independence and outspoken individualism, the last citadel of America's frontier spirit. To others it is a haven for those seeking serenity and sameness. To television and Hollywood the Midwest is the nation's breadbasket, the creator of everything wholesome and healthy. Politicians tell midwesterners that we are the ultimate ratifiers of what constitutes mainstream thinking. (Politicians say that to everyone.)

On the other hand there are those for whom the Midwest is the epitome of narrow thinking—a dull, hard-scrabble place hospitable only to cows and the culturally deprived. Who's going to argue with them?

Midwesterners, that's who. We love a good argument. It's part of our DNA.

"It's in the lack of agreement," wrote Columbia University's J. R. Humphreys in his 1966 book, *The Last of the Middle West*. "It's among all the contradictions that the composite face and figure of the Middle West can be seen. . . . The Middle West can be reached by corridors of conflicting views."

In 1928, *New Yorker* humorist Robert Benchley chided those who would stereotype the typical American. There are no such things, he said, as midwesterners or easterners or westerners or any otherners.

"There are simply dull, solid one-hundred percent Americans," Benchley said. The typical New Yorker, like the typical American, he went on, "has two children and wants them to have a good education. He is 100 percent American, 100 percent business and 100 percent dull. And much as he dislikes New York, he would live in no other place . . . he is the product of no one section of the country but of all sections."

I agree with Benchley about the Heartland. I also agree with J. R. Humphreys and Professor Shortridge and the college students and my friends and neighbors in the Old Settlers Parade. The Heartland is everything American, and everything American is in the Heartland. As much as we dislike the weather and our politicians and our lousy roads and our high taxes, we would live in no other place.

At least I would not. I have counted it an accidental blessing to have lived among people who insist on good manners while nourishing dissent and debate. Midwesterners are the keeper of traditional American norms and values, and the first to thrust their chins into the face of anyone who would use those norms and values to dictate how others should live, worship, or vote.

The Heartlander is a free American—free to speak his mind and take his stand. Even if he's not sure where it is, exactly, that he is standing.

Listening to Voices

Some parents say that all a child needs is love. I disagree. I am not a parenting expert, but I disagree anyway. I'm a midwesterner.

Loving a child is important but it doesn't take much effort. Children are easy to love. So are hot coffee, bluegrass music, basketball, and the chewy center of a Tootsie Pop. If raising happy, contented children were as simple as loving them, the world would have fewer bullies. Even bullies were loved once by someone.

What a child needs is a voice. I didn't invent this theory, but I agree with it. Dr. Richard Grossman probably didn't invent it, either, but he has a Web site about it (www.voice lessness.com).

"Giving voice," says Grossman, a Brookline, Massachusetts, family psychologist, means letting a child understand "that he or she will be heard.

"There is no better anti-anxiety, anti-depressant, anti-narcissism inoculation than this implicit sense of worth," he continues. "Children with voice have a sense of identity. . . . They stand up for themselves when necessary. They speak their mind and are not easily intimidated. They accept the inevitable frustrations and defeats of life with grace and keep moving forward. They are not afraid to try new things, to take appropriate risks. People of all ages find them a joy to talk with. Their relationships are honest and deep."

From what I can tell, my ancestors believed in "giving voice." My aunts and uncles and grandparents were a menagerie of German, French, and Polish eccentrics who immigrated to the Midwest and found it a good fit for their tendentiousness.

My parents, in turn, passed this mouthiness along to me, though it was many years before I knew what to do with it. I was shy and aloof as a child. Maybe I was intimidated by all my loudmouthed relatives.

Eventually I discovered my voice, and I began to use it. I lost my shyness and stopped frowning.

"Speak up," Mom would say. "I can't stand children who don't speak up and talk so you can understand them."

She said this almost as often as she told us those stories about my brother Stephen and the nuns and the first day of school and how she cried when he walked away without saying good-bye.

Loving other people isn't hard work. Listening to them, however, takes practice. You have to practice shutting up. When the room is quiet, you can hear someone else's voice. More importantly, they can hear their own.

The alternative to this, Dr. Grossman explains, is voicelessness. Which leads to fear.

A little fear can be a good thing. It keeps a child from crossing busy streets and getting into cars with strangers. Too much fear—fear of people in authority—is a bad thing.

Nuns in Tennis Shoes

I was in sixth grade before I was aware that nuns wore tennis shoes.

It was the holiday season, 1966. My family attended St. Ann's Catholic Church, a rapidly sprawling parish in a rapidly sprawling Heartland suburb.

After Mass one Sunday morning, my mother drove across the St. Ann's parking lot and into the driveway of the convent where the Catholic nuns lived.

Mom handed me a box of moist dates hand-stuffed with pecans. A holiday treat for the nuns.

"Just go up to the door and ring the bell and tell them it's from us," she said. "No one is going to bite your head off."

Mom was always telling me not to be afraid of people who were not going to bite my head off. *That's what you think,* I thought. *You don't have one of them for homeroom teacher.*

The box of dates in one hand, I pushed the flimsy doorbell button that dangled from its receptacle next to the screen door. The screen door was there, I assumed, to keep small children and other insects away from the handsomely stained mahogany door, the one with the crucifix with a peephole just above Jesus' head. I felt like I was approaching a haunted castle on Halloween.

To the door came my science teacher. I won't use her real name (nuns never told you their real names anyway), but I can tell you it definitely was not Sister Charisma. So we'll use that one. In class she never smiled or made small talk with students. Her right hand was always wielding one of those classroom pointers that look like pool cues. The other hand was used to restrain the noisy rosary beads that dangled from her "habit," the black robe and headgear that hid from view virtually every part of a nun's body except her eyes, nose, and mouth. I always wondered how they could hear through those things.

I had never had any personal contact with a nun outside of school or church. I didn't think they *had* personal lives. I assumed that a Catholic nun's life consisted of grading home-work papers in the day and praying rosaries at night. My best friend David Leavitt told me nuns slept and showered in their habits but I didn't believe him.

Now Sister Charisma was staring at me through the screen door. I couldn't tell if it was a look of surprise or irritation, but I was relieved to see she wasn't holding that pool cue.

Through the screen I also noticed that she was wearing tennis shoes.

Hers were not austere, chaste, and celibate sneakers. These were boys' Keds basketball high-tops. It was convent housecleaning day. Behind Sister Charisma I could see a covey of other nuns scurrying back and forth across the hallway dragging buckets, mops, and rosary beads behind them.

For a second or two, I wasn't sure what struck me the most—that nuns wore tennis shoes or that they did housework without removing those heavy black robes and rosaries. I was beginning to think David Leavitt was right after all.

After giving herself a few seconds to let my face sink in, Sister Charisma surprised me with an extremely toothy smile. Now that I think of it, I had never seen her teeth before, either. She parted the screen door to accept the box of dates. Over my shoulder, she tossed a wave toward my mother. She said the dates and pecans would be a nice snack after she and the other sisters finished the cleaning.

Then she disappeared back into the haunted castle. I mean convent.

"What did she say?" Mom asked, as I slid back into the front seat. I glanced across Mom's lap, through the driver's window, back at the convent.

"Nothing. She just said thanks."

On the way home I realized Mom was right. No one had tried to bite my head off.

⸎

I had this same revelation many times as I got older—not

about nuns in tennis shoes, although they continued to surprise me. Nuns eventually got rid of those thick black robes. Shortly after I got married, six Franciscan sisters challenged me and some friends to a volleyball game at a church picnic. They kicked our butts.

My revelation was the difference between how people behave at work and how they behave at home. Some people—particularly those with power and influence—have one personality they use at work and a different one they use when at home. At work these people have a certain tone of voice they do not use around the house or in the yard.

There is a certain way powerful people walk through doors and sit in chairs when they are on the job and in control of others. When they get home, however, they wear tennis shoes. Away from the office, they are just like everyone else.

Do you suppose NBC's Matt Lauer greets his wife in the morning the same way he greets his interview subjects? Do you think he waits in the kitchen while someone ushers his wife in from a waiting area, pushes her into a stiff-backed swivel chair directly opposite Mr. Lauer, and then clips a microphone to her blouse while he reviews a sheaf of briefing materials? Do you think he subjects her to the same unrelenting, penetrating questioning that we have come to associate with morning network news programs?

LAUER: Good morning, honey.
WIFE: Hello, Matt. How are you?
LAUER: I'm fine. And you?
WIFE: I'm fine.
LAUER: Thanks for being here.
WIFE: Glad to be here.

I don't think so. Matt Lauer probably talks to his wife the same way I talk to mine. It is the same way people everywhere talk to each other when we are just being ourselves, which is to say we are being what Benchley called 100 percent American and 100 percent dull.

ME: Hey. [This is midwestern for "hello."]
WIFE: Hey. [Rooting around in her purse for car keys and lipstick. Does not make eye contact.] Who left this backpack in the middle of the floor?
ME: I don't use a backpack and we only have one child. So take a guess.
WIFE: My, my. Is someone having a bad day?

This is the way normal people talk. At least it's the

way people talk in the Heartland. The Midwest may be full of vast open spaces, but a few of us live there. We live in small worlds. We grow up with the sons and daughters of the people our parents grew up with. We know one another's home voices and work voices and we are not intimidated by either. We know all about voices and how to use them.

It's hard to get to know people if you are intimidated by them, and it's hard to be intimidated by people once you get to know them. Second only to their contentiousness and their big hearts, this is what I like most about Heartland people—their intrepid, in-your-face fearlessness.

Life got easier for me when I lost my shyness, when I realized that nuns and college professors and politicians were not so frightening. At work they may speak in erudite, complete sentences and seem beyond the reach of human scrutiny. But when I see them at the grocery store they are just dull, normal Americans like everyone else. They say goofy things like, "Hot enough for you?" and they read *People* magazine while standing in the "12 Items or Less Express Lane" with more than twelve items in their cart.

They don't seem so scary after all. So I get in line behind them, with fifteen items in my cart.

Questions and Answers

Fearlessness comes in handy in most careers. Whether you're a news reporter, an attorney, or a family physician, your success depends on one thing: how good you are at getting information out of total strangers who are obviously lying to you.

My mother was a fearless interrogator. She could spot a fib the size of a speck hiding under a haystack in the next county.

HER:	Did you put gas in the car?
ME:	Yes.
HER:	How much gas did you put in?
ME:	You asked me if I put gas in the car. I did.
HER:	Did you fill it like I asked?
ME:	You just said put gas in the car.
HER:	I can stay here all day if you want and play word games, or you can answer my questions.
ME:	I think I'll go put more gas in the car.

Mom understood that the key to successful communication is to banish the notion that other people are smarter than you. You have to see them as just more smart-alecky brats who are trying to use your car without paying for the gas.

I became an effective newspaper reporter only after I stopped quaking in the presence of people smarter than me. Early in my career, I would be dispatched to interview some mayor or city manager about his plans to lure new commercial development to town by giving giant tax subsidies to wealthy developers. The mayor did all the talking while I listened and nodded vacantly, making it obvious that I understood nothing he was saying. Usually the toughest question I asked was, "Could you spell your last name for me?"

Thanks to good role models, like my mom and my professors at journalism school, I began to unleash my inner Midwest fearlessness. It totally transformed my style of interviewing.

CITY MANAGER: This shopping mall would be financed with $10 million in special obligation bonds. It is perfectly legal.

ME: Wouldn't you say that *special obligation bonds* is really just a government term for "borrowing money"?

CITY MANAGER: Well, yes, if you want to put it that way. The city is borrowing money to help the developer build the shopping mall.

ME:	And how are these loans paid off?
CITY MANAGER:	With sales tax and property tax revenue generated by the shopping mall.
ME:	So, putting it another way, the taxpayers are helping subsidize a private shopping mall.
CITY MANAGER:	I think that's a very cynical way to look at it.
ME:	How do you spell your name again?

You don't achieve this level of impudence overnight. It took practice. Over time, I began to use that voice my parents gave me. I learned to loosen up in the company of mayors, governors, and chief executive officers. The way I see it, what I want to ask is just as important as what they want to say.

If they refuse to answer my questions, they will regret it later. I'll send my mom over, and they'll have to answer hers.

Pistol Packin' Prairie Publishers

If you think Midwesterners are outspoken today, you should meet our ancestors.

As a Kansan I come from a long line of journalists who carry a certain name-calling gene that is passed from generation to generation. The result is that I am inexorably, biologically compelled to carry on the hell-raising tradition begun by my rugged newspaper ancestors who spent much of their time insulting each other.

I am a pussycat compared to the nineteenth-century prairie journalists and editors who preceded me. The 1800s was a time of blustery newspaper wars in the Midwest, and name calling was a prized art.

During the early 1850s Thomas J. Key, editor of the *Doniphan Constitutionalist*, dueled frequently in print with archrival publisher Sol Miller of the *Kansas Chief* at nearby White Cloud, Kansas. The following are actual editorial excerpts.

"We would gently hint to the cross-eyed, crank-sided, peaked and long razor-nosed, blue-mouthed . . . empty-headed, snaggle-toothed, filthy-mouthed, hammer-hearted, splaw-footed abolition editor to attend to his own affairs or we will pitch into him in earnest," editor Key editorialized one day.

Editor Miller, fighting fire with fire, replied: "We said his name was Thomas Jefferson Key. We beg Thomas Jefferson's pardon—it should have been Thomas Jack-ass Key! No insult intended to jackasses generally."

These journalists had what one Kansas historian called "tremendous vocabularies." These pioneer publishers were hotheaded, vituperative wordsmiths who ignored the line between press freedom and personal freedom. In doing so, they laid the groundwork that later would make it possible for America's journalism profession to boast the tallest headlines in the free world (ROSEANNE'S CHILD IS HALF GERMAN SHEPHERD!!).

The *Kansas Historical Quarterly* cataloged some of these early newspaper wars in a 1944 article titled "Pistol-Packin' Pencil Pushers." Among those was an 1889 rant by *The Jacksonian* in Cimarron, Kansas, whose publisher apparently was ticked off by something he read in the competing *Ingalls Messenger*: "We are onto the lop-eared, lantern-jawed half-bred and half-born whisky-soaked, pox-eaten pup who pretends to edit that worthless wad of subdued out-house bung-fodder, known as the Ingalls Messenger."

On May 16, 1868, the *Marysville Enterprise* described the editor of a competing paper as a "red-headed, frizzleheaded, mush-headed, slab-sided brainless deformity and counterfeit imitation of a diseased polecat." *

And the *Eminence Call* in 1897 rendered this tribute to one of its local newspaper rivals: "He, of course, was not responsible for the fact that he was born a complete degenerate and fitted out with a face that causes children to scream with fright and old, staid farm horses to break their halters and run away when they see him coming toward them. Those who have known him from childhood say that the first sentence he ever uttered was a lie and since then he has never told the truth except on compulsion."

Kansas historian Don Wilson, in a 1978 essay, "Barbed Words on the Frontier," noted that the men who ran these papers had one thing in common—they were never neutral about anything. "Their language doesn't wiggle, wobble or waver, beat about the bush, put out a smoke screen, play hide and seek or dodge the issue," Wilson wrote. They said what they meant and meant what they said.

Does this mean that I think newspapers and reporters should use such colorful language today? Should I describe the actions of the state legislature or the city council as "outhouse bung-fodder"? Get serious. There haven't been outhouses around here for sixty years.

---

*It is no longer considered in bad taste to refer to a Kansas publisher as a diseased polecat.

It means it's not my fault that I am so prickly and caustic. I cannot help the way I write. It's inherited.

THREE

EVERYDAY TRIAL, EVERYDAY ERROR

Hard Lessons, Soft Landings

My dad never hurried. He drove under the speed limit. When assembling a toy or fixing an appliance, he would spread the parts and instructions on a flat surface. Then he assembled, one step at a time.

When hanging a picture frame, Dad used a measuring tape and a carpenter's level. It drove Mom crazy.

"Always go back and check your work," he said. "Go too fast and you'll make mistakes."

My father was right. Most of the mistakes I ever made in my life were the result of hurrying. Some of these had severe consequences. In other cases I was just lucky.

I was rushing to get dressed for work and get my son ready for the nanny. He was six months old.

One of us needed a diaper change, this I could smell. I hauled him into the master bedroom and plopped him on the bed. As I began to dislodge the currently-in-use diaper, I realized that all the diaper-changing supplies were down the hall in the baby room.

It would have been smarter to lift him, bare bottom and all, tote him down the hall, retrieve the diaper tools, and start all over. This is what my father would have done.

I was in a hurry, so here is what I did. I left the baby on the bed and dashed down the hall to fetch the supplies. I wasn't gone but fifteen seconds when I heard the thump. It's amazing how much of a thump a naked, well-fed baby makes when he klonks to the ground from a four-foot perch.

The distance from the baby's room to the master bedroom is about 20 feet, and I covered it in one heart-stopping leap. I flew through the doorway and looked down to see my son lying flat on his back, staring up at me. It was one of those looks that small children make in the first nanoseconds after a mishap, during which time they are processing what their brain is telling them, what their body is telling them, and what the look on your face is telling them, and then using all this neurological data to decide whether to cry or laugh.

The *holy-shit* look on my face at that moment must have resembled one of the goofy clown faces I often made while tickling and tossing him. He pumped his chubby fists across his chubby chest, as if he were applauding, and squealed with glee. I swear to God.

I held my infant boy for a long time that morning, and I was extremely late for work. He and I agreed we would not tell his mother what a bonehead thing Daddy had done, at least not for about seventeen years.

Never again have I left a baby unattended on a bed, although once when Max was seven my wife spotted him riding his Big Wheel in the middle of the street when I was supposed to be watching him. She still brings this up at dinner parties.

That was the old me. The current me works slowly, especially around babies. Like my dad I choose the slow and sure route over the fast and painful one. I drive under the speed limit and I read assembly instructions carefully before beginning. When hanging a picture, I use a tape measure and carpenter's level.

It drives my wife crazy.

Directions for Dads

I attended a business luncheon where the keynote speaker explained why people like me are not wealthy. He said people like me are always in a hurry and always guessing when it comes to important decisions. This, he said, leads to bonehead impulse decisions that produce unhappy consequences, like what happens when you leave an infant unattended on a bed.

The speaker recommended that people like me appoint a personal board of directors to oversee our finances. This panel of advisers would consist of accountants, lawyers, and consultants who would meet with me quarterly, as a committee, to review my estate and balance sheet, much as a corporation's board of directors meets with its management.

No thanks. I have enough brokers, insurance agents, and accountants in my life. Whenever I visit with these geniuses about my money, I can never shake the sensation that we're talking not so much about goals for me as we are opportunities for them.

What I need is an advisory panel for fathers. This idea is not as stupid as it sounds.

The average dad arrives at this job a clueless blunderbuss. Our fathering instinct is a *tabula rasa*, a blank slate destined to remain free of practical information. Even when we do learn something useful about raising children, we immediately forget it because something else requires our attention. There is too much to remember. One minute we're learning how to take an infant's rectal temperature, the next minute we're figuring out how to apply the lawn's winter fertilizer. Extra nitrogen.

My accountant tells me what I need to know about 1040s and 1099s. I have SEPs and IRAs. What I need is a BODD: Board of Dad Directors. The board would establish goals and objectives based on a time line—what to do when my child is five, when he is ten, and when he begins to drive or date. For example:

DAD'S MANAGEMENT OBJECTIVES FOR SEVENTH GRADE

1. Volunteer to coach his basketball team.
2. Skip your gym workout on Tuesdays and Thursdays and help him with homework.
3. Get tougher about practicing the saxophone.
4. Forbid him to stay out past midnight on weekends.

The BODD and I would have monthly meetings. There'd be coffee and coffee cake, easels and three-piece suits. PowerPoint bar graphs would measure my progress, assuming I had made any. Overhead transparencies would document how much money I spent on designer basketball shoes and games of laser tag in the past month, compared with how much I had saved for his college. I would give a status report summarizing my fatherly gains and losses, the pain and the profits. A secretary would take minutes.

At year's end I would present highlight videos and annual reports. There would be scenes from family holidays and vacations, soundtracks from family arguments. The directors would sit there and nod with pity, the way you look at someone trying to swim upstream in Jell-O. Afterward they would pepper me with tough questions, like how often I told my son yes and how often I was strong enough to say no. Like a good CEO I would take credit for the successes; for my failures I would blame the economy.

With any luck my Board of Dad Directors will treat me the way God will treat me, or at least the way I hope He will. I don't subscribe much to the notion of a punishing God— one who dangles me by a frail thread over a hot flame, just waiting for me to screw up so he can drop me into the fire. That kind of God seems too much like a human being, or a plaintiff attorney.

I prefer to think of a helpful God, one who not only points me down the right road but also goes along for the ride to make sure I don't miss the turns. This Board of Dad Directors would possess godly patience. Its members would be rocks of the profession, the best fathers in the business. They would succor and soothe. They would focus on the bottom line while I shouldered the details.

That's the kind of direction parents need. We want reassurance that we're making the right moves. We also want an incentive plan. If my kid turns out well rounded and polite, doesn't run off with a religious cult, and gets a scholarship to a good college, there should be a big bonus. Maybe extra sick days or vacation time.

I am well aware that the know-it-all competent fathers out

there will snipe that my idea is for sissies. They will say that a Board of Dad Directors would suck all the spontaneity out of parenting, that it would strip the guesswork from the time-honored tradition of fathering by trial and error. If someone held your hand and told you what to do during every child-raising crisis, you would never learn to stand on your own two feet. You would never experience the anxiety and heartache that is a critical part of the learning curve for a clueless parent.

The more I think about this idea, the more I like it.

Our Father, Our Protector

I would have learned more about parenthood if I had spent more time watching my own dad and less time watching television.

Instead, much of my information about fathering came from observing Theodore Cleaver's father on *Leave It to Beaver*. I was led to believe that the job consisted mostly of sitting around the house all day in a suit and tie, reading a newspaper, and waiting for your wife or kids to ask you for money. I don't recall anyone mentioning that a father must sacrifice himself to shield his family from danger.

Anthropologists say the male's protective instinct can be traced to prehistoric family units. Before the Jurassic Family would bathe in the river, Mrs. J would ask her husband to wade in first and make sure the water was safe. If Mr. Jurassic wasn't eaten by a giant anaconda, the family knew the water was safe. If he was eaten, it was still safe because the snake wouldn't be hungry again for another four or five hours. The males fell for this every single time, which is why, over a couple of million years, Prehistoric Protector Father eventually evolved into Ward Cleaver.

The concept of Dad as Live Bait has changed little through the ages, unless you count a brief period during the late 1960s when, thanks to the feminist movement, women insisted on proving that they could do anything a man could do. This was a tragic historical blunder, as women discovered that a guy is more than happy to let his wife handle whatever chores she wants around the house as long as she doesn't ask him to get off the sofa and kill a giant snake or anything.

Even a lazy father, however, cannot escape his destiny. I learned this the hard way—not from television, but by getting married and having a child. My wife, a liberated woman who can do anything a guy can do except drink dill pickle juice straight from the jar, announced one day that she had bought an antique lamp and repaired it herself.

"I rewired it," she beamed like a sixth-grader who had just won first place in the school science fair. Then she handed me the lamp. "It was easy. Can you plug it in and see if it works?"

Looking back, I should have asked some technical questions. *If she rewired the lamp and was confident of her liberated-woman electrical skills, why is she asking me to test it out? Why is she standing clear across the kitchen right now crouching behind the cooking island? Aren't you supposed to re-install this little piece of insulating cardboard so the wires don't make direct contact with the metal casing when you flip the . . .*

I haven't seen such a huge ball of flame belch from such a tiny appliance since the time Michael Weaver set a beaker of kerosene on Father Fahey's Bunsen burner in tenth-grade chemistry class. It happened so fast I barely had time to notice that a buzzing sensation was rocketing through my left hand, which was still gripping the lamp. My wife, who in addition to being a skilled electrician is also a trained health care professional, alertly ran to my side and shouted, "Did you scorch the hardwood floor?"

Such exhausting demonstrations of my Family Protector skills usually reduce me to a quivering gelatinous mess, and all I can think about is how nice it would be to lie on the ground and dab my burns with antibiotic ointment. But the minute I relax, some new evil threatens my loved ones.

The creekbed in my backyard is a popular summer destination for vacationing snakes. Snake tourists in baggy Hawaiian shirts often slither out of the creek, plop down tiny lawn chairs, and sit back to watch the fireworks coming from our house, cheering as huge balls of electrical flames bolt from the kitchen appliances. One day, one of them slithered up for a closer look.

PHONE CALL
FROM HYSTERICAL
BOY CHILD: Dad! Dad! There's a huge black snake in the garage! Can you come home right now?

FATHER: Calm down. The snake does not necessarily want to bite you. He wants to bite somebody but not necessarily you. I'm at work right now. Just take a broom and shoo it into the yard.

HYSTERICAL
CHILD: No way! I shut the garage door and trapped it in there. I called Mom, and she said to call you!

It was apparent that, like civilizations of fathers before me, I would have to protect my family. Arriving home, I calculated the odds. My opponent was a snake. I was an upright human and therefore, technically, a superior species. The reptile had razor-sharp fangs, deadly venom, and a powerful tail capable of knocking its enemy senseless. On the other hand, I owned a faulty lighting appliance that, through no fault of mine, was capable of emitting huge fireballs at the flick of a switch.

Now, before anyone writes nasty letters about cruelty to animals, let me assure you that the snake didn't feel a thing.

I think. It was over in a flash, so to speak. Well, the snake was still squirming a little, so I grabbed a shovel and . . . Never mind. I was shaken, but my fatherhood was intact. My family was safe.

I glanced up and saw my son standing in the doorway. He was looking at me the way you would look at a person you saw walking through a shopping mall with a vacant stare and a chain saw. My wife said his nightmares would probably stop after a few sessions with the school psychologist.

As for me, this Protector Father thing is getting easier as time goes on. Nowadays, whenever my son and wife need me to fix an appliance or fend off an invading creature, they just handle it themselves.

Meetings of the Minds

Now that my son is old enough to drive, we don't talk as much. My chauffeur time used to be our talking and sharing time.

I miss the days when he needed me to drive him to school, home from school, to birthday parties, back home from birthday parties, and so on. Tooling around town together afforded us time for those heartfelt conversations that a child can have only with his mother or father.

Conversations might be the wrong word. What a six-year-old boy has on his mind in the backseat of a car is not necessarily what's on his parent's mind in the front seat. The child's head is racing with questions about the latest bits of informational shrapnel that were picked up that day on television or the playground. The parent's mind is a combat zone of unfinished errands and unresolved dilemmas.

It's too bad there's no way to record these parent–child "conversations." I'll bet space aliens can do it. I'll bet aliens have powerful electronic eavesdropping gizmos that let them monitor what humans on earth are saying and thinking at all times. I'll bet they listen to our on-the-road conversations and then they try to compare what the child is saying out loud in the backseat to what his parent is thinking in the front seat.

I'll bet *heartfelt conversations* never occurs to them.

SON: Daddy did you know Jason Dalton can get to the fifth level on X-Men? Who would you like to be? Wolverine or M. Bison? Daddy do you think Scottie Pippen is taller than Michael Jordan? Can we go over to Josh's house and shoot baskets? Who do you want to be? Celtics or Bulls? I'm hungry.

FATHER: [thinking] *I'll just tell the sales guy to fax me the quote on the new car. I'm not going over there to listen to his stupid sales pitch . . .*

SON: What does Bart Simpson mean by that? Daddy? Look look look. Do you think this is a scary face? Jennifer Wolcott says my faces are stupid. Can you call her mom or her dad and tell her to be nice to me? Daddy? She got her name on the board three times and her parents said if she got her name on the board again she can't have a birthday party . . .

FATHER: *The Visa balance is $1,700. Need to pay something on it . . . get the front lawn mowed . . .*

SON: Can we go to Applebee's? You said we could! Daddy what's a coma? If I die first will you and Mommy be there? Can you do anything you want in heaven?

FATHER: *Was I supposed to turn the oven off and put the casserole in the fridge or take the casserole out of the fridge and turn the oven on?*

SON: Matt said my Barry Bonds card is only worth fifteen cents. Do you think it's worth fifteen cents? How much do you think it's worth . . . Daddy, Mommy said that for a special treat, since I'm going to go to the doctor to have my ears checked, she would take me to Baskin-Robbins . . .

FATHER: *Jeez, look how fat my neck is getting. I gotta get back on the NordicTrack . . .*

SON: Daddy, how many seconds are in a day? Does a coma hurt? I am worrying a lot about having a coma. I don't want to go to gymnastics tonight. My legs hurt. Do I have to have my eardrops tonight?

FATHER: *. . . If I get home by 6:00, and get the new grass seed down . . . Move the peony bushes . . . Maybe if I get pizza and a video he'll take a nap . . .*

SON: Daddy, how many seconds are in a day? If I got a dollar every second for a day how much would that be? Daddy? How much would that be? Would I be rich? Can Tricia come over and play?

FATHER: *. . . Maybe if I reboot from the startup CD and turn off all the extensions, then reinstall the print driver . . .*

SON: If I could be an animal, I'd want to be a dolphin. Would you want to be a dolphin? What's faster—a dolphin or a cheetah? I need to know!

FATHER: *. . . Aw [very bad word]. I was supposed to get a baby-sitter for Saturday night . . .*

SON: Josh taught me some new words to the Barney

song, Daddy. Listen. Listen, Daddy. Daddy? "I hate you, you hate me, let's team up and kill Barney . . ." Wouldn't it be awesome to have a dolphin? You said we could go to Applebee's.

FATHER: *Two columns to write by Monday . . . How come she always makes me get the baby-sitter?*

SON: Daddy? Daddy? What's the fastest animal? Wow! Did you see that car? Wasn't that awesome? Would you like a car like that, Daddy? Who's taller? Tricia's dad or Michael Jordan? Daddy? Daddy?

FATHER: *. . . I need to go home and lie down.*

SON: Daddy?

Pets and Paying Attention

"There is no nice way to say this," said Dr. Gray, our family's veterinarian.

He had my attention.

"It's her anal glands," he said. "Most dogs have them. Hers smell really bad."

Those may not have been the doctor's exact words. All I remember is, "It's her anal glands somethingsomething-something . . ." Then I went pale.

63

A few months earlier, my wife had noticed that Cayman, one of our two yellow Labrador retrievers, was scooting around on her butt. Kathy said that she—the dog—would pull her hind legs together, squat low, and then drag her butt on the ground. Like a penguin.

"Something is making her bottom itch," my wife said. "We need to take her to the vet."

I can see all you experienced married persons nodding right now. You know that when your spouse says that "we" should handle some unpleasant task, it really means "you" should do it. You know this because you have been married a long time and your parents were married a long time and any married adult who does not understand these things by now clearly has not been paying attention. However, if you do not know which are the "we" tasks and which are the "you" tasks, do not worry. Your spouse will explain it to you.

<hr/>

So there we were, me and an extremely agitated sixty-pound Labrador retriever, in an exam room the size of an elevator. Suddenly the veterinarian blurted out the words "anal glands."

Being a guy, I activated the same facial expression I employ when the car mechanic recommends something that sounds like "replacing the O-rings." I rub my chin and nod as though this is exactly what I suspected and that I am now weighing the merits of replacing the O-rings as opposed to, say, shampooing the carpets.

Dr. Gray noticed me rubbing my chin and continued. Dogs, he said, have two glands way down there by their you-know-what. Over time, these become repositories of bacteria powerful enough to destroy the Brazilian rain forest. These are the same "scent glands" that skunks use to scare away their enemies. In a Dog v. Skunk Gland Shootout, thousands of innocent bystanders would perish.

Mother Nature put these vile organs on a dog's behind because she is not very bright and she thought this would keep them from sniffing each other's rear ends. This idea backfired. It turns out that the worse something smells, the more a dog is attracted to it. Your typical Labrador retriever will not even consider chasing one of those doctor-recommended, tartar-removing synthetic bones you buy for him at the store. But grab a handful of raw sewage from the storm sewer and wad it into the shape of a bone and he will pounce on it as though it were a Polish sausage.

Now here's the really interesting part, Dr. Gray said. Other than causing an itchy bottom, foul odors, and huge veterinary bills, a dog's anal glands *serve literally no biological purpose whatsoever*. I suppose Mother Nature thinks this is very funny. Dr Gray certainly did.

To remedy the itching, Dr. Gray explained, there are three options, each one more revolting than the other:

1. Get rid of the dog and get a cat.

2. Choose surgery. The doctor removes the glands, the contents of which—I cannot emphasize this point too much—must be shipped off to the Nevada desert, lest they fall into the hands of an international terrorist organization.

3. Perform an at-home "maintenance" procedure on the dog that is so hideous I can't believe Dr. Gray even brought it up. Each time he attempted to demonstrate this maneuver, Cayman would attempt to launch herself off the exam table and through the closed door.

As the old saying goes, "Let sleeping dogs with bacterial infections remain heavily sedated." So I chose surgery. It was easy and painless as far as I was concerned. Cayman, however, came home from the surgery humiliated and sore. Later that afternoon, our other Labrador took a break from chasing balls of sewage around the yard and sauntered over to sniff Cayman's surgical incision. Cayman nearly ripped her head off.

My dog no longer does the Penguin Walk, but sometimes she bites her toes. With pets you're never sure what they are trying to tell you.

The next time something is bothering my dogs, I will pay more attention. If I think it involves some gruesome infection that calls for a visit to Dr. Gray, I won't procrastinate. I will march upstairs and tell my wife it's her turn.

Everything a Dog Needs to Know

We may not always pay attention to our pets, but our pets always pay attention to us.

Your dog, for example, thinks about you all day. Specifically, he is wondering how many hours it will be until you feed him again. A dog, like most people, wants nothing more than for someone to pay attention to him. Unlike many people, however, a good dog knows how to get attention—and how to keep it.

I sat down with my oldest and wisest dog, Cayman, and asked her about this. She explained that everything a dog ever needs to know is not learned in kindergarten or obedience class or even on public television. It is inherited. Dogs are born with a preexisting awareness of the commandments for personal contentment. They have a sixth sense for getting along, as unfailing as the instinct for remembering how to find a bone buried before the last snowfall.

Most dogs adhere to these commandments. Some do not and, as a result, are grouchy and ill mannered; they bark endlessly for no apparent reason. Just thinking about these pathetic creatures makes Cayman sad. If only they knew what she knew.

I wrote down the commandments as I understood them. No explanations or amplifications are available. All I know is what my dog told me.

THE RULES OF CONTENTMENT

- Unlike many humans, never pretend to be something you're not. There is no greater calling than caninehood. This is as good as it gets.
- Always eat your food quickly and in gulps. They'll think you're starved and let you have seconds. (Cats have never learned this.)
- When someone is having a bad day, be silent. Sit close by and nuzzle gently.
- After a bath shake with all your might.
- When your master says, "Sit!" it's okay to wait until he says it a couple more times to see if he really means it. When it comes out, "SIT!!!!!!!" then park your fanny.

- Learn how to shake hands with humans. This is awkward and unnatural for creatures without thumbs, but it will endear you to small children and people who need cheering up.
- If urgent circumstances force you to piddle in the wrong place, such as on someone's guitar case, don't blame yourself. It doesn't hurt, however, to crouch nearby with your head on your paws and look contrite.
- Thrive on attention. Let people touch you. Sit very close to them and always lean in a little.
- To determine if people are true dog lovers, quickly roll onto your back. If they scratch and rub your tummy, you can trust them.
- On walks sniff enthusiastically at everything you pass. Show your boundless zest for the outdoors.
- Bark only if barked at. Ignore peaceful creatures like birds and rabbits. They are no threat.
- Ignore those who say that leftover barbecue ribs or angel food cake will give you a stomachache. We are dogs. We have stomachs of iron.
- If the master makes a move toward the walking leash, drop whatever you were doing and nearly knock him over as you make a beeline for the door.
- When given a new chew toy or biscuit, devour it

with glee. You'll probably get another.

- When they come toward you with the food bowl, prance in circles and wag your entire body. This makes them laugh.

- Always engage in some minor, neurotic behavior when your owners are gone for a long time. This lets them know you missed them. Peeing on the porch rug is one way. Ripping out the rhododendron bushes, however, may push your luck.

- Don't pout after being scolded. Run right back and show them you love them anyway.

- Always snore contentedly when taking naps on the cool kitchen floor. With any luck, they will let you sleep there all night. When you awake, lower your head and stretch your front paws as far as you can reach.

- Treat every hug, every pat on the head, and every tummy rub as if it were the best one ever. In all things, let them know that no dog ever had it so good.

Big Dreams in Small Ponds

The only thing midwesterners love more than their dogs is fishing. I know people who take their dogs fishing, but most of them (the dogs) have little patience for it. If a dog has nothing to chase and no raw sewage to eat, he takes a nap and calls it a day.

A fishing enthusiast, however, never calls it quits. Whether fish are caught or not is beside the point. The point is the fishing. There is no past tense. There is only the present and the future. One is never fished out or done fishing. As long as there are lakes and ponds—and the Heartland is freckled with them—there is fishing to be done, now and forever.

My friends Steve and Tracy are bass-fishing addicts, although that term is too weak to describe the level of their interest. Steve and Tracy enjoy bass fishing more than life itself. They certainly love it more than eating or sleeping. On the night before our annual Memorial Day fishing trip, Steve doesn't go to bed. He remains upright all night in the cabin recliner, with one eye on his video of *The Fugitive*—which we watch seven or eight times every trip—and the other eye on his tackle box.

My angling skills are limited to accurately attaching the three-day fishing permit to the lid of my tackle box, so I always fish with Steve and Tracy. My number one rule when it comes to outdoor recreation is, "Always go with people who know what they are doing."

The best way to spot an experienced fisherman is by the size of his tackle box. Steve and Tracy each have tackle boxes the size of a Weber grill. Open one of these behemoths and you behold a sprawling, multi-level bait condominium that smells like it was used to transport skunk carcasses. Inside are little round lead things ("line weights") and hooks ("rigs") and bait ("lures"). Tracy always brings a Gerber's jar filled with bull semen, one whiff of which reportedly makes a wide-mouth bass swoon with desire and which I hereby submit as evidence that there are creatures even more repulsive than dogs, olfactory-wise. My own tackle box is an old Sucrets throat lozenge container that also holds my guitar picks.

Steve arms himself for fishing the way a golfer stocks his arsenal of clubs. There are rods for every situation: a rod for big fish, one for small fish, one for topwater fish, one for fish that vote Republican, one for odd-numbered days of the month, and so on. When nothing is biting for me, I just caddie for Steve. ("Sir, I believe this shot calls for the twenty-pound-test line with the Texas rig-caster hunchie spinner three wood.") Tracy works at a grocery store so he brings the sunscreen and beer. I always bring the snacks for the boat, which consist entirely (I kid you not) of Peanut M&M's.

On my trips with Steve and Tracy, I learned that there are two basic techniques for pond and lake fishing:

Technique 1. Stand in a $30,000 bass boat all day without catching anything.

Technique 2. Stand on a mosquito-infested bank of weeds and cattails all day without catching anything, returning occasionally to the boat for more beef jerky.

Regardless of which method you use, the fish will stay way the hell clear of your lure and laugh hysterically at the ridiculous gizmos attached to your line. Trust me, a five-pound bass has been around long enough to know that a purple-and-white plastic "worm" with spinning metal blades and a POWERBAIT logo is not a naturally occurring lake organism.

No matter how experienced you are, it never hurts to spend $150 a day for a professional fishing guide. It never helps, either. A general rule is the more BASS PRO and BASS-CAT corporate decals on his boat, the more likely your guide is to have his fishing show on cable television, which is what he'd rather be doing than trolling around a lake all day unsnagging your hook from underwater tree limbs.

Professional or amateur, if you fish long enough you'll soon develop your own tricks and techniques. Tracy swears to God that it's possible to catch large fish by putting nothing but a spray of WD-40 on the hook. Don't laugh. At Lake Fork, Texas, one of the nation's most famous bass-fishing venues, Tracy's name is inscribed on the wall at Val's Marina Cafe as the only person in Lake Fork history to fish for twenty-seven hours straight and catch nothing but a grotesquely overgrown catfish.

This is not to give you the impression that Steve and Tracy and I fish all day without catching any fish. Usually we fish all morning and afternoon without catching any. Then sometime around 8:00 P.M. after having had nothing to eat all day but Peanut M&M's, someone whips his line backward, causing that sharp *swoosh* that means he has set his hook into a big one.

The battle begins. Hearts pump and muscles tense. The line jerks and darts as man and fish square off in an underwater tug-of-war. The rod is bent over as though it were made of rubber. Someone reaches for the hand net. Peanut M&M's go flying all over the boat. At last a defiant yet majestic-looking bass—covered with WD-40—is hoisted by the bottom lip. Poses are struck; snapshots are taken.

This is what fishing addicts live for. At least it is what Steve and Tracy live for. For them fishing is like having a baby. It is long hours of anticipation following by a few frantic minutes of pushing and pulling. The payoff is a fleeting moment of exhilaration in which you proudly hold aloft this small, slimy miracle for all your friends to admire. Then you throw it back in the water and keep on fishing. You know you should quit, but you cannot. You don't remember all the work and the waiting because all you remember is the exhilaration.

Tracy and Steve will never quit. In the Heartland there is always a lake or pond calling them. They will go fishing whether I go with them or not, but they would rather have me along. I always bring the M&M's.

Blessed Are the Good Listeners

There are two ways to learn:

1. By making mistakes;

2. By listening to people who have made more mistakes than you have.

Personally, I found it a lot easier to make mistakes than to listen. I would have made many more had it not been for good teachers. My mom taught me how to stand up for myself, and my dad taught me how to fix appliances and hang pictures. Dr. Gray taught me about dogs, and Steve and Tracy taught me how to fish. I can only imagine how much more I would have learned—how many mistakes I might not have made—had I paid better attention to people smarter than me.

So when my son got in trouble at school one day for not

paying attention, I decided not to talk about it. We could have had a heartfelt, father–son conversation, but why bother? He wouldn't have listened. He's just like his father.

Instead, I wrote him a letter. I figured he can read it when he's older, when he is wondering about all the things I told him when he wasn't listening.

Dear Max, my son:

I am sorry your fourth-grade teacher made you cry today. Apparently, you asked her to explain something she had already explained to the class. She told you she wasn't going to explain it again, and then she told you to sit down.

Mrs. Finklehaus seems like a good teacher, Max, and a nice one, too. Sometimes children—and adults—don't listen well. Part of Mrs. Finklehaus's job is to teach you to listen so you don't make unnecessary mistakes.

One day you'll see how right she was.

The biggest mistakes you will make over your lifetime will be the result of not paying attention. Bad listeners always get the instructions wrong, even simple ones like "shampoo, rinse, repeat." Thanks to Mrs. Finklehaus, you'll do things right the first time. And you'll have a clean scalp.

People relish the company of good listeners, Max. Be a good listener and you will never be lonely.

Good listeners have a sixth sense for when to make a point and when to be still. They do not interrupt, even when the other person is disagreeable or mistaken. People don't mind being corrected as long as you first listen to what they have to say.

Many people who might have been your enemies will rally to your side because you listened to them when no one else would. The best way to get people to mistrust you is to correct or criticize everything they say.

In your career you will be promoted over others because your listening skills will get you to the bottom of a problem faster than your peers.

Small children will love you and cherish your company. Grownups lose the respect of children not by disciplining them too much, but by listening to them too little.

Good listeners know how to communicate with God. The reason many people find no comfort in prayer is because they do all the talking. They never shush up long enough to hear what He is trying to tell them.

One day a splendid woman will fall in love with you because you are such a good listener. Each night before she falls asleep, she will thank God for sending her a companion who is good at pillow talk and pillow listen. Because of you, she will fear neither the dark of night nor the arrows that fly by day.

Listening will bring you love, Max. And love will get you through the darndest things you could ever imagine.

Thanks for listening,

Love, Pops

The Painkiller

"David! David! Can you come here?"

The clock radio on the nightstand said 4:47 A.M.

"David . . . I need you. Can you hear me?"

I saw that there was no one in the bedroom but me. The voice was coming from the hallway. A ribbon of light was seeping under the door and lighting up the carpet.

Shoving my glasses onto my face, I opened the door and looked out. My wife was standing at the end of the hall, her back toward me. She wasn't moving.

"David, can you come here?"

"Kathy?"

She had almost made it to the linen closet, which also is the medicine closet. She heard my voice but did not turn around.

"I'm sorry. I can't move. It's my back."

Kathy is a family physician of osteopathic training. She knows her musculoskeletal structure the way a field general knows his battlefield. She knows pain and all its hiding places.

"It's the L3 and probably the L4," she said, more for her own benefit than mine.

Her spine was taking revenge for a weekend of bad posture. On Saturday there had been a wedding (sixty minutes in wooden pews) and a reception (two hours in cafeteria-quality plastic chairs). Saturday night had been our son's high school production of *Oklahoma!* When your kid has a big number in the school musical, you attend all three weekend performances. The next morning was choir rehearsal and Sunday Mass. More wooden pews and plastic chairs.

By Sunday night Kathy's lower back had been under attack for nearly thirty-six hours. After she went to bed, the muscles and ligaments retaliated. Under cover of darkness, land mines of inflammation were planted along the spinal path, the heaviest concentration near lumbar discs 3 and 4. When the nociceptors in the brain signaled the counterattack, her peripheral nervous system unleashed a blitzkrieg of pain. The neurons in her brain gave up without a fight.

I tried to rotate her back toward the bedroom.

"Ho," she said. "Slower . . . Ooh, my God."

The family physician in her wanted to run tests and order consultations. The patient in her wanted to pop a couple thousand Advil and climb back in bed. I could see in her face that doctor and patient were having an argument.

"You're going to have to take me to the hospital."

Forget that, I thought. *I can't even get you down the hall.*

"First I need to use the bathroom."

Dozens of baby steps down the hall, one foot in front of the other.

"I'm sorry, Babs," she said. "I'm sorry you have to do this."

<hr>

We had always called each other Babs. It was from the Peanuts cartoon strip, where the love-struck Sally was forever wooing Linus, the aloof bachelor.

"My Sweet Baboo!" Sally would cry out as Linus fled in horror.

<hr>

I led Kathy into the toilet room off the master bath and had no idea where to stand, where to put my hands, or where my eyes should look. She was staring at the floor, so that's what I stared at. In your entire life, I thought, no one teaches you how to lead your invalid spouse to the bathroom, strip off her clothes, and stand over her while she pees in front of you. Then you have to kneel at her ankles and hoist her underwear into place as she sobs only partly from the pain and mostly from the embarrassment.

I made an effort not to reveal how conscious I had become of the pale flesh, the body hair, or the odor of urine. I cursed myself because I could think of nothing to say to relieve the pain or the embarrassment.

"You'll be fine," I said.

Kathy stared at the floor and I realized she was not fine. She was in terrible pain and all I could come up with was, "You'll be fine." Dumb, dumb, dumb.

<hr />

If this were lovemaking, I would not feel so clumsy. Any man can undress a woman. But try lifting her from a dead toilet squat without bending her at the waist. Try reattaching her bra without twisting her arms, or figuring out which side of the pantyhose is the front and sliding it over her toes without raising her feet. It feels like diapering a baby, but at least there was training for that. In the nursery they let you practice on dolls that don't cry or pee.

The next two hours was a series of ordeals accomplished at a pace near the lower limit of what constitutes human movement. The nineteen stairs from the bedroom to the first floor. The sidewalk from the front door to the car. The parking lot from the car to the hospital.

The staff at the hospital's Pain Management Clinic had just unlocked the doors when we arrived. She was seen right away, a professional perk. A doctor does not wait in another doctor's lobby. The doctor's husband does, but not the doctor.

A nurse named Melinda helped Kathy down the hall. Another one named Cody came toward me with a skeleton doll. Running her fingers down the doll's spine, she explained that an "epidural" is technically not an anesthetic but the place where the anesthetic is injected.

A long needle is inserted into a space—called the epidural space—just outside the last of the three membranes that cover the spinal cord and just inside the bone and ligament. The needle makes a hole in this space, through which a soft catheter is threaded. The needle is removed, the point of entry sealed, and the catheter taped to the skin. Through the tube, measured doses of anesthetic are delivered to the lower spine. Hello, la-la land.

"It's *wonderful* when you're having a baby," Nurse Cody said.

I thanked her for the show-and-tell and skipped the urge to mention that my wife was a family doc with a C-section scar and a bad back. I'd heard it all before.

I knew about anesthesia but not about relieving pain. I hated the fact that I had felt so clumsy that morning, that I had not known how to care for my wife or console her. It made me feel incomplete, like an unfinished sentence. Had Kathy noticed my awkwardness? Did it frighten her? Did she wonder what it would be like in twenty or thirty years when she needed me to feed her, bathe her, or wipe her? Where do you learn how to do this? Does anyone ever get good at it?

I recalled that my mother was good at it, but she'd had a nurse's training. She was as dauntless around vomit and bedpans as she was around the kitchen pots and pans.

"You just do it," she had said. "You don't think about it. You just do it."

⋯⋯✕⋯⋯

An hour later Kathy walked through the waiting room door. It was more of a shuffle than a walk, but she was flying solo and smiling. On the elevator ride down to the lobby, she kept telling me that I was the best husband in the world.

"I think the epidural has gone to your head," I said.

Or maybe it was me. Maybe I was her anesthesia, the clumsy husband who had done nothing more than stand there and love her and tell her everything was fine and that even if the pain doesn't go away he will not and, because of that, she does not have to be afraid. If all it takes is love, I felt I could be good at this.

Maybe love is like anesthesia. Neither one repairs the injury; it just takes away the pain—and the fear. Isn't that why we kiss a child's pinched finger? The kiss doesn't fix anything. It merely erases the child's fear that the finger will always hurt the way it does right now.

⚜⚜

"Thanks, Babs," Kathy said as we returned home and began retracing the steps from the driveway to the front door. "I'm sorry you had to do this."

I told her there was nothing to be sorry for. "It was good practice for when I have to visit you in the nursing home."

She poked me pretty hard for someone who was heavily sedated. Still, I could see that her energy was seeping away like air squeaking from a popped balloon.

"I think I want to get back in bed now," Kathy said.

I knew what was coming next.

"But first, will you help me use the bathroom?"

⚜⚜

I did, and it wasn't so clumsy this time. Then I tucked her in bed and she slept the rest of the day.

⚜⚜

FOUR

EVERYDAY TEARS

When Families Weep

American literature has reached the point where average, middle-class families have all but vanished. At least you never read about them anymore.

Novelists and screenwriters seem incapable of depicting a family that doesn't include at least one alcoholic father who hates his job and batters his wife, one or two promiscuous daughters who hate their mother, one womanizing son who is stealing from his boss, or a borderline psychotic mother who is having an affair with a neighbor. I don't know many people like this, but I imagine it would be interesting to spend the holidays with them.

Most of the families I know are less interesting and definitely less entertaining. They harvest crops, wait tables, teach high school biology, and work in health clinics and law firms. They shovel snow, rake leaves, coach baseball, volunteer at church, and spend their lunch breaks composing "to do" lists on napkins. Their garages are so crammed with bicycles and lawn mowers that they must park their cars on the driveway all winter. They don't speak in carefully constructed sentences because they have too many things to say and too little time to say them. Their favorite expressions are "yep" and "no problem." They do not rescue the world from terrorists or space aliens on a daily basis, and most of them do not photograph well (the wind and humidity in the Midwest do terrible things to your hair). They expect strangers to speak courteously but are quick to forgive those who do not. They do not get huffy or impatient if someone steps in front of them in the checkout line. They were taught to believe that you never walk out on marriages or children, even bad ones. They work long hours and at day's end can barely summon the energy to drag themselves to the bedroom, whereupon they flop facedown on the pillow and thank God that nothing terrible happened to their children this day. If you catch them in a mathematical moment, they will tell you their lives are 90 percent family, 10 percent church, and 100 percent unlike the families of popular literature. The latter estimate is a gross exaggeration.

The families of fact and the families of fiction have one thing in common: They all look the same when they cry.

Wealthy or working class, all men and women get the same suffocating sensation in their chest when they lose a job or their life savings. Every mother and father crumples into the same puddle of flesh and bones when the emergency room physician explains that a son or daughter has died in a farm accident, a car wreck, a tornado, a flood, or a shooting. Every child who has lost a parent goes to sleep at night asking God to let him wake up in the morning and find that this was all a bad dream.

Tragedy is what all families have in common. It is what makes them normal, even the galactically dysfunctional ones. How they cope with tragedy is what sets them apart.

The families of fiction don't have to cope with tragedy. They have authors and copy editors to it for them. There are plot twists and flashbacks, but everything comes out fine in the last chapter. The handsome but flawed hero always gets a second chance *and* the pretty girl. The planet is always saved and tomorrow always comes. There may be tears along the way but the readers must have a happy ending, the publisher must have a best-seller with spin-off film contracts; the author must have a review in the *Sunday Times* that heralds a "rousing story of hope and redemption!"

In real life, misery has less company. There is no copy editor to wipe away a mother's tears or console a grieving father. There is no *deus ex machina* or Clint Eastwood to save them from what threatens to knock them down.

When Everyday People suffer, they must rescue themselves. They do this by remaining connected to family, friends, and God. None of this makes them interesting; it only makes them resilient. What sets them apart from the people of literature and fiction is not so much what happens to them but how they handle what happens to them.

Everyday People survive because they wake up every day and hear voices.

"Here we are," the voices say. "We are your friends and your family and your God and we will always be here for you. No matter what happens, we are here."

Fragile Birds

Mark Huston's family could not save him, but he did not blame them. How could he?

The best days of his life were the ones spent as a little boy with his mom and dad and two sisters. He loved his world then, because it was small. His world was his parents and two sisters and his yard on the shady cul-de-sac in suburban Kansas City. Just beyond his backyard was a neighborhood park with soccer fields and playgrounds and big shade trees—giant oaks, walnuts, elms, and ashes—that were ideal for climbing.

The house and yard and the park were Mark's safe, small world. Given a choice, he never would have left. He would have stayed a little boy in a little world.

But Mark had grown up. He had grown into a tall teenager with big fears and worries. He tried to make the worries go away, but he could not. His family had tried, too, but they could not. Everyone had tried and tried, because everyone loved Mark.

It was no one's fault, least of all his family's, that although Mark had grown very tall, he still felt very small.

So fifteen-year-old Mark Huston got out of bed in the middle of the night on August 28, 1995, a few days into his sophomore year of high school. The day had been uncommonly hot, even by Midwest standards. It was *To Kill a Mockingbird* hot. Like the heat in *Midnight in the Garden of Good and Evil*.

Midwest nights are cooler than the days, but not by much. The air was thick with mosquitoes as Mark walked out the back door of his house and across the backyard. He walked through a gate and into the park, the one with all the big shade trees. It was dark but he knew the way. This was his small world.

Mark stopped at the foot of one of those trees. He wrote a letter to his parents and sisters, thanking them for all the good times they had given him. He reminded them that he loved them very much and that none of this was their fault.

Then Mark climbed into the tree and hanged himself with his own belt.

This is not a story about suicide or bipolar disorders or

teenage depression; I have no credentials in such things. It is a story about the difference between happy people and frightened people, between normal families and tragic families. You don't have to be an expert to know what the difference is. You don't need to be a psychologist to know that sometimes there is no difference at all.

"I always felt if you do what you're supposed to do as a parent, you would always have your kids around you," Cindy Huston told me seven years later, on another hot August day, sitting across from me in a Kansas City coffee shop. "Things may not be perfect, but you would have the relationships with them that you want.

"To me, that was almost like a guarantee."

For a long time life was perfect for Cindy and Dave Huston. They had done all the right things. They lived in an affluent Midwest suburb and sent their three children to the best public schools. A lifelong midwesterner, Cindy knew about hard work. A former schoolteacher, she knew that raising children was hard work. She and Dave worked hard and got what they wanted: three beautiful children.

Carrie, Mark, and Jessica were like most siblings. They were alike and different at the same time. They were birds from the same nest, each with its own personality and voice.

All three were bright. All three seemed happy. They played well together. But Cindy could tell there was something extra special about Mark.

"He was such a sweet little boy," Cindy said, drawing out the word so it came out *sweeeeeet*. Mark had a tender heart. He loved his sisters and his parents. Anyone could see that Mark loved everyone. He even loved school—at first.

Later on, Cindy said, it was obvious why Mark loved his first few years of school. School felt like home. First and second grade are warm, safe places where everyone plays nice, no one judges you, and the teachers give hugs and kisses.

Because he loved school and his teachers, Mark excelled. He was intellectually gifted, everyone said. Mark liked being smart. Smart kids get love and attention, and no one enjoyed *that* more than Mark the Sweet.

"On his papers in first grade, he would write to his teacher, 'I love you,'" Cindy said. "And his teacher always took the time to write back, 'I love you, too.'"

As Mark pushed through fourth and fifth grade, Cindy and Dave noticed that he was different from his sisters in one other respect. Like many bright children, Mark was extremely sensitive. His feelings were easily hurt by things that other kids seemed to ignore. In first grade teachers hug you and put happy-face stickers on your papers. In fifth grade teachers can be petty and uncompromising; friends can be fickle and hurtful. Mark could tell he wasn't in second grade anymore.

Cindy was concerned, but she had a plan. She was a former teacher with special-ed experience. She knew about children with special needs. You have to pay close attention to them.

"Whenever I'd come home, I'd always make sure that I asked about his day, or asked how school went," Cindy told me. "He'd always say, 'Fine, Mom!' Just like that. He would always say he was fine." Her son was Mark the Fine.

I told Cindy my son says that, too. He's about Mark's age. I call home and ask about his day and he always says it was fine or great. Never any details, just fine. Thinking about this was a distraction. I tried to focus on Cindy.

"We all do that, don't we?" she said. "We see their happy faces and we think they're happy. We figure that if something was wrong with them they'd look miserable all the time."

My son's face popped into my head again. I have no idea what a normal, happy kid looks like if he's actually miserable. I can't think about this right now. Focus, focus.

There is one other thing that bright kids do, especially bright, sensitive kids. Sooner or later they develop a defiant streak. Smart Midwest kids are like their smart Midwest parents. They ask questions and they want answers. Sometimes they get contentious. They want everything to be right or wrong, black or white. They have trouble seeing the middle ground.

"Their eyes," Cindy said, "are like the lenses of a camera. They take in all this information about life and love and friendships and disappointments. But their hearts are still small. They can't process everything they see. They have all these questions."

Some days all the questions backed up in Mark's mind like a clogged sewer. He would strike back. As he approached junior high, Mark began to confront principals and challenge teachers. If punished, he would question the punishment.

"Around the playground, the kids called him Mark the Brave," Cindy said.

The world, however, is not black and white. It is gray and inscrutable, and a scary place for fragile souls. Kay Redfield Jamison, author and psychiatry professor, has written that depressed, frightened people are the dry kindling of humankind, walking atop the embers but unable to handle the sparks life throws up. Mark's two sisters seemed to dodge the sparks just fine. Why couldn't Mark?

Mark preferred the days when there were no sparks. "In ninth grade," Cindy said, "he sometimes would go by and visit his second-grade teacher."

The mother dove raises all her children in the same nest. She feeds them all the same and teaches them the same lessons about the dangers that lurk on the ground. Most of her chicks grow strong and resilient. They learn when to fly from danger and when to stay and defend themselves. But inevitably one of the chicks is not strong. Its wings are fragile and its legs are weak. It is not strong like the others and it cannot defend itself. One day it topples from the nest. It does not last long on the ground, where nature has little mercy on fragile birds that cannot defend themselves.

<hr />

Near the end of ninth grade, lots of people were trying to save Mark. Psychologists told Cindy and Dave about teenage depression and adolescent hormones and bipolar disorders and chemical imbalances in the brain. This led to counselors and medications. There were alternating episodes of tranquility and terror, signs of progress followed by signs of deterioration.

The Hustons had walked into every parent's nightmare. Your child is giving you all these signs but you don't know what they mean. What if you miss the signs completely, or misread them? It was like looking at the pieces of a jigsaw puzzle, Cindy said, or peering through a kaleidoscope. Every time she and Dave looked inside Mark's head, they thought they saw something else.

"I knew he was in pain, but I thought it was temporary," Cindy said. "I thought I could fix it. It made me feel like a mother."

Psychologists say there is a Rubiconian line between depression and hopelessness. Depression can be treated because it can be seen. Hopelessness, however, transforms its victims. Their minds go numb and they appear deceptively tranquil. Friends and family see a human mirage; the hopeless person sees the end of the struggle.

As he began his first week of tenth grade in August 1995, Mark crossed the line. Thanks to counselors and medications and the constant love of his family, he seemed to be getting better when he had actually gotten worse. It was the start of a new school year, when kids are excited about new beginnings and new opportunities.

Mark Huston didn't feel excited or new. He felt like the same old Mark, which meant he felt like an outsider, someone who didn't fit in. To him, the world was no longer a safe place. He was no longer Mark the Fine, no matter how often he said he was.

The worst part for Mark, Cindy said, may have been the fear that he had become a burden to those who loved him the most—his family. After all, his parents and sisters had given him the best days of his life, his childhood. His own pain was bad enough; now he was causing theirs. Mark didn't want to be remembered that way. He wanted to be remembered as Mark the Sweet, the gifted child of Cindy and Dave, the loving brother of Carrie and Jessica.

That's the memory Mark wanted to leave behind the night he died, the night he wrote the letters to his family at the base of the tree in the park behind his house. He wanted them to remember how much he loved them. He wanted them to know that everything was fine now, the way it used to be when he was little. Tonight he was going to be Mark the Brave and make the fear go away.

"I had seen the signs," Cindy said. "We were talking and we were trying to help him. It never really sank in that I, with all my special-ed and counseling experience, I could lose my boy."

Cindy didn't get weepy when she said this. She gave me her stern, Midwest schoolteacher look. At teachers' college she must have majored in Strong Eye Contact.

"Do not think that it can't happen to you or anyone else," she said.

I listened and thought again of my son. I couldn't help it.

"There are no guarantees," she continued. "You have to take advantage of the good times that come and love people when they are here, while you can. That's what hit me in the face after losing Mark. I think that's why I wasn't nearly as shocked by the September 11 tragedy as other people. It didn't surprise me."

It didn't surprise you?

"No. But everyone else seemed so surprised. They couldn't believe that such a terrible thing could happen. But I believed it. When you've had the worst possible thing happen to you, you know that anything can happen. You know there are no guarantees."

There was more I wanted to ask Cindy, and I could tell there was more she had to say. We agreed to save it for next time. She wanted to get home to her husband and daughters. I wanted to get home to my son; I wanted to ask about his day.

Cindy headed for the door. I packed up my laptop and tape recorder and left the coffee shop.

As I walked outside into the summer sauna, I could see that ashen clouds were trying to blot out the afternoon sun. In the distance there were quick flashes of lightning and soft rumbles of thunder. No one reached for umbrellas; no one paid any attention at all.

Lightning and thunder are normal on Midwest summer afternoons. It could mean that a severe storm is on its way, or it could mean nothing at all. You never know what the sky is trying to tell you.

Just One Second

Greg Hill pushed back from the cocktail table in the lounge of the Capitol Plaza hotel in downtown Topeka. He told the other dads at the table to keep an eye on his beer. He'd be right back. He wanted to kiss his kids good night.

Greg had already kissed them good night a couple of hours ago. But it wasn't enough. He could never get enough of his wife and kids.

Upstairs in the hotel room, Kathy Hill and her four children were winding down from an evening in the hotel pool. The Hills were in Topeka for son Shawn's soccer tournament. Tomorrow they'd be heading back home to Olathe, Kansas, about 100 miles away.

Greg returned to the room, inserted his key, and turned the knob. The floor was a minefield of clothes, drinks, trash, and temporary beds. Shawn, ten, was on a roll-away bed. Kaitlyn, twelve, and Maggie, six, lay on a sofa bed. Five-year-old Jack was in bed with Kathy.

The room looked like it had been struck by a Kansas tornado. Greg loved it. He was the kind of dad who didn't mind messes and commotion and noisy children and crowded hotel rooms. He didn't see a mess. He saw his family.

The children were awake but fading fast. Their heavy eyes were laced with sleep and swimming pool chlorine.

Without saying a word, Greg leaned over to Shawn and spent a few minutes scratching his back. Then he did the same to the other three, stepping from bed to sofa to cot. The kids loved it when Greg scratched their backs. It felt good to see Dad's face before falling asleep.

Greg felt the same way. A father needs to see his children's faces before he goes to sleep.

Then Greg told Kathy he'd be right back. Just one more beer with the other dads. He wanted to get a good night's sleep. Tomorrow was a big day—Shawn's last soccer game and then the trip back home to Olathe.

And one more thing.

Tomorrow was Mother's Day: May 12, 2002.

"What do you think made him come back up to the room that night?" Kathy asked me eight months later, as we sat in a Starbucks talking about that weekend in Topeka and how it had changed her life. "He could have stayed out late with the other dads and the kids would have gone to sleep with me. But he came upstairs to tuck them in.

"Do you think he knew . . . ?" Her voice trailed off.

"Happy Mother's Day!" Greg said, bear-hugging Kathy from behind on the sidelines of the soccer field. It was the last game of the day. It was the last time Greg would ever hug his wife. Then the six Hills piled into their Mercury Villager minivan and headed back to the hotel in downtown Topeka, to pack and check out.

Greg was driving; Kathy was in the passenger's seat. Behind them in the middle seats were Kaitlyn and Shawn. In the backseat were the little ones, Maggie and Jack.

"It was cold and rainy that morning," Kathy said. "I remember looking back and the kids were sitting in the center of the seats with only the lap belts. I really didn't like that so I made them move apart and sit over against the doors so they would have the shoulder harnesses."

It was drizzling, but Greg could see just fine as he turned the van onto eastbound I–70 back toward the hotel. He could see his kids in the rearview mirror. He could see from the dashboard clock that they would have enough time to get back home, attend Sunday Mass as a family, and then make it to his sister's house for a Mother's Day dinner.

Greg could see that this would be the best Mother's Day ever. He also may have seen the Jeep Cherokee up ahead, coming toward him on the other side of the concrete barrier that separated the eastbound and westbound lanes of I–70.

Chances are, however, that Greg did not see the deer.

⚊⚊✕⚊⚊

The chances of a deer darting across a roadway in the Midwest are as good as the chances of spotting a family in a minivan heading home from a soccer game. Kansas logs about 10,000 deer–car collisions a year, but fewer than 5 percent of them result in human injuries. And only a fraction of those result in deaths. Most deer–car collisions occur around dawn or dusk and mostly on rural roads; most occur in the fall. The Hills were on an urban interstate at midmorning in mid-May.

All the chances and odds went haywire on May 12, 2002, just after 9:40 A.M. There are 86,400 distinct seconds in a day and something like 2.5 billion seconds in an average life. At this particular second a deer that had wandered onto the westbound lane of I–70 was sideswiped by a Jeep Cherokee driven by twenty-five-year-old Kimberly Schwanke. The Cherokee struck the deer with such force that the animal's head was instantly severed. The remainder of its body was launched over the barrier that separated the lanes of traffic. Its headless carcass came crashing back to earth in the eastbound lane at the same second that the Hill minivan was passing in the opposite direction.

Kimberly Schwanke was not injured. Greg Hill, forty-two years old and father of four, was pronounced dead at the scene.

Whether Greg died instantly isn't certain. A passerby who rushed up to the minivan claimed that, just before closing his eyes, Greg turned his head toward the back of the van—toward the kids. A father needs to see the faces of his children before he goes to sleep.

Kathy suffered severe injuries to the socket of her left eye, her nose, and her jaw. When she and I met at the Starbucks in Kansas City, three more surgeries were pending.

The children were spattered with animal blood and fur, but unharmed. After it crashed through the van's windshield, the deer's decapitated body had rocketed down through the center of the minivan like a divinely guided missile. It slashed a path precisely through the center of the backseats—the unoccupied space where the Hill children had been sitting only moments earlier.

"If I hadn't moved the kids over to the door seats a few minutes earlier . . . ," Kathy said. She paused to see if I had caught her drift. I had. "Don't you think there's a certain order in life? Don't you think that things sometimes happen for a reason?"

I told her I did. I said I couldn't speculate on what Greg knew the night before he died, when he left his buddies in the bar and came upstairs to tuck the Hill kids into bed. I said Greg probably did that because that's what good dads do every day.

Being a good father had always come naturally for Greg Hill. Kathy thinks he learned it at home. Good fathers raise good sons, who grow up to be good fathers. A couple of years before the accident, Greg's father had become ill and unable to operate the insurance agency he owned. So Greg quit his law practice, obtained an insurance license, and took over the family business. He did it for his father.

"He thought his dad's health might improve," Kathy said. "He wanted to make sure the agency stayed in the family, just in case his dad wanted to come back to work." She added that Greg was just like her own father: "Dad always arranged work so that he was home when we were there. It was important to him to swing with us in the backyard and watch TV with us or come to our games. He worked very hard, but he arranged work around family. Mom said that sometimes after we all went to bed he would go back to work."

I told Kathy it was easy to see the cycle. Kathy's parents and Greg's parents believed that family was more important than work or money. They taught this to their children, who taught it to theirs. Now Kaitlyn, Shawn, Maggie, and Jack were learning what their mother and father wanted them to know—the importance of staying close to family. Kathy and Greg came from big, close Midwest families. In such families, kids may grow up and move away, but never very far. They stay close enough so that aunts and uncles and grandparents can be there for birthday parties and soccer games and graduations. And funerals.

"My sister put her own life on hold and just moved in with us. She told her own family that they'd just have to get by without her for a while." Kathy said her brothers were currently helping the four children build a playhouse for the backyard.

"Who does that for you except your family?"

No one, I said. No one but family.

Kathy snapped the lid back on her carryout coffee cup and said she needed to get home. It was Christmas break and the kids were out of school. I asked how the children were adjusting to life without Greg.

"Their faith has been very strong," she said. "When we go to the cemetery, there is never a tear. They always say, 'It's not Daddy there in the ground. He's still with us and we'll get to see him again in heaven.'"

She gathered a scarf around her neck.

"That's our faith," she told me. "We believe that somehow God will make us strong enough to do this. It happens one step at a time. Then one day you tell yourself, *I can do this. I can really do this.*"

I believed her. Kathy Hill was going to do this. An improbable, random instant of tragedy had taken her husband and her children's father, but it had not taken everything. She had her children and her faith; she had her children of faith. She had memories of a good man who taught her the most important lesson of all.

Greg Hill knew that it was not enough to love your family. You must tell them. You must kiss them and tuck them in bed and scratch their backs every chance you get. Just in case it's the last chance you get.

The Mourning After: Normal Never Returns

"We die every moment."
—St. Paul

Exactly one year after America's September 11, 2001, terrorist tragedies, the anniversary memorial ceremonies are on television.

It is easy to see that the victims' families gathered in New York City today are in as much pain today as they were a year ago—as much pain as they will be next September and the September after that.

For them, life will not resume. Nothing will be normal again.

The thousands of grieving New York families have

joined the family of millions who suffer and grieve every day, in every town, and on every continent. They are in every home and village. Those who have had loved ones snatched away suddenly understand what the World Trade Center families now understand.

Grief never sleeps. These families cannot be consoled; they can never return to normal.

"I knew what they were going through," Kathleen Turner of Oklahoma City told the *New York Times* as she described how she felt upon hearing about the World Trade Center attacks. Turner's four-year-old daughter, Ashley, perished in the April 19, 1995, bombing of the Alfred P. Murrah Federal Building in Oklahoma City.

"I knew what they were going to go through for years and years. You never get over it."

In author Sue Miller's *While I Was Gone*, a minister delivers a homily at a friend's funeral. He tries to explain the therapeutic value of vividly recalling another person's life: the way she danced, the way she tipped her head when she laughed, the time she cut off all her hair.

"Pain is part of memory, and memory is a God-given gift," the minister says. "Loss brings pain, yes. But pain brings memory. And memory is a kind of new birth within each of us."

Those who grieve find solace in the memories. They do not want to get over it. They do not want to "heal." They didn't have some disease. They had a mother or father, a sister or brother, and now there is only a gaping hole in their lives where these people used to be. Survivors don't want to get on with their lives. This *is* their life, grieving and remembering.

September 11, 2001, was a worldwide tragedy, so the families received worldwide comfort. Across the planet, complete strangers sent prayers and money. The vigils and wakes and candlelight memorials continued for a year and will continue for years to come.

The world is not so comforting to everyday families who suffer everyday tragedies. There is a simple funeral followed by a week or two of flowers and sympathy cards. Friends pitch in and church volunteers deliver casseroles. It is all a blur and it is over in an instant. The cards and casseroles stop, but the pain does not. The grieving are expected to recover and get back to normal. Whatever that means.

Normal life is the worst part. The grieving do not want to go on with whatever it was they were doing. They drive down the street and they want to shout out the window, "Hey! What's wrong with you people? How can you go back to school and your jobs and your baseball games and Christmas parties and your family reunions? Don't you understand that life is not the same anymore?"

It would be wrong to suggest that those who grieve are bound and gagged by hopelessness. Many are brave, resilient people who do what resilient people always do. They reach out to something stronger than themselves—they reattach themselves to family and church and community. Having found new meaning in death, they discover new meaning in life.

Those who find new meanings will eventually laugh again. One day they will be able to remember their loved ones with a little less pain. They will be able to get through the grief, one day at a time, one foot in front of the other. They will cope and adapt. But their lives will never be normal again.

No Relief

Life never did return to normal for the Chartrands; it simply quit hurting. Twenty years after Eddy died and Arthur lost his job, the good times had begun to outnumber the bad ones, though sometimes by the slimmest of margins.

Broken marriages and cracked careers had been mended or replaced. Family photos now brimmed with in-laws and grandchildren who had come along in the years after those terrible days in 1979. Then in the spring of 2001, Arthur learned that he was to receive a considerable inheritance from his younger brother.

Hubert Chartrand was diagnosed with acute leukemia in January of that year and died on April 17. To no one's surprise, he had refused chemotherapy. Even at seventy-four, Hubert was a fit and vigorous bachelor with an insatiable appetite for literature, European history, French poetry, classical music, and travel. He wanted a life of conversation and exploration or no life at all.

"My advice for you," Hubert told my son, Max, during one of our last visits to his hospital bed, "is to try everything there is. Taste it all." Then he lifted a frail arm and waved. *"A la prochaine fois!"*

One of the most fundamental of human needs, I suppose, is the need to find a meaning and shape to tragic events in order to justify them. Maybe the meaning is there, or maybe we just want to believe it's there. As much as Hubert's swift passing saddened us, it was impossible not to be struck by the paradox of tragedy as a healing, redeeming influence on our lives. Eddy's death in 1979 had revivified our family twenty years ago and brought us closer together. Now the bittersweet inheritance from Hubert meant that Arthur and Christianne would, for the first time in twenty years, be delivered from the ignominy of constant financial worry.

As we mourned Hubert's death and toasted his life, an unspoken sense of liberation came over the family. It felt like Arthur, Christianne, and the much-expanded Chartrand family were being given a second chance at having what most families want—dull, normal, everyday lives. It didn't feel like happiness as much as it felt like relief.

The feeling lasted about twenty-four hours.

———

Two years earlier, Stephen Chartrand had contracted something called autoimmune hemolytic anemia. It's an insidious disease that deceives the body into attacking its own blood cells. Steve's breathing became labored; his face and eyes became jaundiced.

Many months and many steroid injections later, my brother seemed to have recovered. We weren't surprised. He was a physician who went to work every day on a campus full of physicians—Creighton University in Omaha. He was chairman of the Department of Pediatrics. He specialized in infectious diseases, and so did his colleagues. If you had to be sick, this was the place to be.

On April 17, 2001, I called Steve's office at Creighton to make sure he knew about Uncle Hubert. His secretary said Dr. Chartrand wasn't in. He was over at the hospital. He wasn't checking on patients, she said. He had checked himself in. Then she transferred me to his room.

Steve answered on the first ring. He said the breathlessness had returned. He told me not to tell Mom and Dad. He didn't want them to worry—not now, while they were getting ready to bury Uncle Hubert. He said he didn't want anyone to worry. He said he'd be fine, but he wasn't sure if he would make it to Kansas City for Hubert's funeral.

Then a nurse came in to check his blood pressure and Steve said he had to go. He'd try to call back tomorrow.

The next morning, all hell broke loose in that hospital room. By noon Steve was dead.

———

April 19, Omaha. I had to get up from my typing and close the door. The women sobbing in the hallway made it hard to concentrate.

Every few minutes I would catch one of them peeking in at me. "Looks just like him," one of them whispered. "Look . . . from this angle. Just like him. God . . ."

This was his nerve center, a windowless bunker that confronted you with floor-to-ceiling bookcases and harsh fluorescent light. The only furniture was a gargantuan government-issue worktable drowning in a sea of medical journals, slide carousels and grant proposals. Everything was where he had left it, less than forty-eight hours ago.

There was a palpable energy here. You just knew he was going to bound through the door any second, in a fury of sound and motion, scooping up notes and slide carousels, late again for a flight and another guest lecture. Boy, wouldn't he be shocked to find me, his look-alike brother, sitting in his chair and tampering with his mail. Writing his obituary.

The closed door had done little to muffle the sobs wafting in from the hall. Here on this medical school campus, these people were his family. Students, colleagues, secretaries. So they did what families always do when tragedy happens. They held each other and wept as a family.

<hr />

April 18, Kansas City. The day before. We seized the first exit ramp off northbound I–29, just north of Kansas City. The road to Omaha. Two cars and four frightened adults: me, my wife Kathy, sister Nancy, and brother Art Junior. We had hit the road the minute we got the phone call from Margie, Steve's wife.

Something had gone wrong in the hospital room, Margie said. She'd have to call right back.

A few miles north of the city, the cell phone rang. It was Margie again. We were too late, she said.

We pulled the cars into a service station and everyone got out. It was one of those moments when time stands still, like the hands on an unwound clock. I don't remember anything but the sound of loud crying and the feel of my brother's thick arms around my neck.

"We have to turn back," Art said. "We gotta tell Mom and Dad." Then we thought of Steve's kids.

Stephen Arthur Chartrand, fifty-one, the first born of Arthur and Christianne's seven children, was the father of four daughters and a son. Two of the girls were to be married in a few months. We should have been thinking about them, but all we could think of was Arthur and Chris.

"We gotta go back and tell Mom and Dad," Art Junior said again. "This is gonna kill them."

⸺⸺⸺

Whenever someone asked my parents why they had seven kids, they would answer, "Because we couldn't have eight." Art and Chris Chartrand like big families. They believed that a large family served a purpose. The more children you have, the more your life has purpose. You take care of your kids when they are little, then they will grow up and take care of you. Cindy Huston told me the same thing that day at the coffee shop when we talked about what had happened to her son.

If you do what you're supposed to do as a parent, you'd always have your kids around you. To me that was almost like a guarantee.

There are no guarantees. Bad things happen every day to good people, people who don't deserve it. Art and

113

Chris didn't deserve to lose a son in 1979, and they damn sure didn't deserve to lose another one now in the spring of 2001, just when it seemed that life was starting to get fine again.

"I suppose life will go on around here, but I don't see how."

That was the first thing his secretary, Carol Maveus, said when I walked into my brother's office: the office of the chairman, Department of Pediatrics.

"Everything you see here exists because he existed," she added. And I believed her.

During the blur of the next three days, I learned other things about my brother, things that did not surprise me, from friends and coworkers. They stood in torturously slow lines to grieve as a family, with our family. This was a man, they told us, who never said no. If he didn't have the time or money, he said yes anyway. Then he found the money and the time. He did it, they said, because all friends were his brothers and sisters, and all children were his sons and daughters.

"You can go in now," my wife said, motioning to us from the doorway of my mother's bedroom. "She just got out of the shower."

Conversations with my mother usually begin before you enter a room and continue well after you've left it. She can talk to you from up two flights of stairs or across a large yard. The minute she knows you're there, she starts talking and never stops. If you try to leave, she just talks louder. It's as though she's afraid that if she pauses for a breath, you might leave and not come back.

As Art Junior and I stepped into the room, she was already on a breathless roll. "I didn't know you two were coming I just had to jump in the shower I was in the garden and my hands and neck were filthy I don't know where your father is he never tells me where he's going are you two hungry? I think we have some lunch meat . . ."

She wheeled around and caught our faces. Hers contorted and she froze, the way people do when you pour cold water down their back. We hadn't said a word yet but she knew this wouldn't be good. She's a mother.

"Your father?"

I knew she'd say that. She fell in love with my dad fifty-one years ago and ever since then has dreaded the thought of losing him.

"No, Mom. Dad's fine." That was only technically true. He was fine because he didn't know yet.

We pulled Mom over onto the love seat at the foot of the bed. Art Junior and I knelt down and leaned over into her lap. We were her little boys again. The world had broken our hearts and we had run home to tell our mother, to ask her to make it all better.

I cupped her face in my hands.

"Look at me, Mom," I said. "We have some very bad news."

Then we held each other for a long time and we cried. Because we are family.

FIVE

EVERYDAY LAUGHTER

Getting the Point

To the Hopi Indians of the American Southwest, laughter is a serious subject.

"There is a natural healing property about laughter," said Lance Polingyouma, a Hopi Indian with a fetching smile and a ready laugh.

I met Polingyouma in Scottsdale, Arizona, where he works at a local cultural center, teaching visitors about Hopi customs and traditions.

"Laughter teaches you how to live," he said.

Polingyouma was not talking about one-liners or the stand-up comedy of popular culture. Secular comics and comedians have no vested interest in the people or institutions they lampoon. Their goal is entertainment, laughter for the sake of laughter. The Hopi people, on the other hand, use laughter to teach the ones they love.

Central to the Hopi teaching tradition is the concept of the Tsuku. The word means, technically, "a sharp point"— like the tip of an awl. It is no coincidence that *Tsuku* also is the name for sacred Hopi clowns—specially ordained teachers who use dramatic exaggeration and parody as a way of preserving tribal discipline.

"In our culture," Polingyouma said, "the family and social roles are very specific. For example, your father does not discipline you. He provides for and protects you. At home your uncles discipline you. On the societal level, it's the job of the Tsuku to correct you."

The Hopi clowns, with their mud-painted faces and bodies, are a combination of jester, priest, and shaman. They appear at ritual ceremonies known as katsina dances. The clown's humorous saber is thrust at those who have wandered astray of Hopi customs, those who need a reminder about cherished norms and traditions.

"That's where the sharp point comes in," Polingyouma said. "The Tsuku pokes fun at people to show them the error of their ways."

When the Tsuku pokes, everyone laughs. They laugh and laugh. Until the clown pokes at them.

"Everyone laughs at the folly of the characters," Polingyouma said. "But it is funny only until a person realizes the joke is about them. Then they stop laughing because it hurts. It's supposed to hurt."

Unlike Hollywood or television laughter, the Hopi laughter cuts both ways.

"When clowns point out flaws and errors," Polingyouma said, "they are also talking about themselves. They are flawed, just as you and I are flawed. We all must laugh at ourselves sometimes because we are all clowns. I am a fool and you are a fool."

As laughter instructs the Hopi family about life, it also teaches about death. Hopi burials, Polingyouma said, are supervised by males of the family. One of their duties is to instigate laughter—blessed, healing laughter.

"At the burial site you are encouraged to laugh," Polingyouma explained. "We don't cry at a funeral. Our people believe that mourning holds back the spirit of the deceased—holds him back from his journey to the underworld. By laughing, we let go and allow the spirit to go on."

The Hopi do not laugh about death, he said. They laugh about life. "We laugh to remember the person positively and the good things they were part of."

I told Polingyouma that some might find it surprising to find such hope and optimism among a people who have known mostly poverty and hard labor. After all, how much humor can you find living in the Arizona desert and trying to farm in a place that gets maybe 10 inches of rain a year?

It is no surprise at all, Polingyouma said. The cheerful heart girds the Hopi for struggle and inoculates them against despair. As the farmer goes into his field, he sings only good songs. He wants all bad thoughts out of his head. The farmer laughs. He knows his plants will absorb his good thoughts. His plants are his children; he wants their nourishment to be only good things.

"We are much like the midwestern farmer," Polingyouma said. "We are simple people, honest people. We choose hard work and struggle because it teaches us how to live . . .

"Yes, life is very heavy. Our lives are serious. Anytime we can laugh, we are making life better for ourselves."

I told him that I was beginning to see that humor wasn't just about laughing; that it had many uses. It can instruct the young, discipline the reckless, comfort the grieving, humble the arrogant, and nurture the weak.

Come to think about it, I told Polingyouma, some of the toughest lessons I ever learned also turned out to be the funniest things that ever happened to me.

"See?" Polingyouma said. "That means you got the point." And he chuckled at his little joke.

The Devil (My Brother) Made Me Do It

I didn't know it in 1973, but the Hopi Indians are right about joking around. Jokes can backfire; then the joke is on you. Sometimes it's not funny until later—much later.

Which brings me to the Halloween prank we played on Helen Stockman in 1973. Helen, in retrospect, was a poor choice. She scared easily. This was a frail, pale sixteen-year-old Midwest schoolgirl who freaked out during fire drills at school.

The Exorcist had just hit theaters. It is still, in my expert opinion, the scariest movie ever made. The scene where Reagan, the possessed girl, spins her head around and the demon inside her hisses, "Reeeaaagan, Reeeaagaan! I want youuu!" remains one of the most frightening images ever to appear on screen.

Helen Stockman had just returned from vacation at the time and hadn't heard anything about *The Exorcist*. As a joke I convinced her to see the movie with me by telling her that it wasn't very scary. I told it was really a dark comedy. Helen was even more gullible than she was frail.

My brother Art, who is possessed by demons, persuaded me to add a few extras to the caper. He would follow Helen and me to the theater. While we were inside, he would smear "blood" (ketchup) all over the steering wheel and windows of my car. Actually, it was my mom's car: a blue Pontiac Grand Safari wagon with a four-barrel "rocket" engine. Mom let us use it on dates, as long we didn't go far. You could *hear* it suck gasoline as you drove and watched the fuel gauge move.

Being typical, insensitive teenage boys, we didn't stop

there. We also made a little tape recording. Art had an old LP of Halloween shrieks, howls, moans—the kind of noises you'd hear at any congressional hearing involving Supreme Court nominations. With the shrieks and howls playing in the background, we overdubbed my voice sneering, "Hellll-en! Hellll-ennn! I want you!" adding lots of reverberation and distortion to make it sound spooky (though others insisted it sounded more like George Burns with strep throat).

The plan was that, just before the movie ended, Art would plant the tape player under the front seat of the car. He recorded just enough blank space at the beginning of the tape to give Helen and me time to get into the car before the sound effects would start.

Looking back on it, I was too young to know you should never deliberately make a redheaded sixteen-year-old girl's heart stop beating. When we got back to the car after the movie—it was very dark by this time—Helen spotted her name signed in "blood" on the windshield. She began to shriek and hyperventilate. It sounded just like Art's Halloween sound-effects album.

Persuading Helen to relax and get in the car did not help. Brother Art, the demon perfectionist, had used ketchup to paint the satanic "666" symbol on the dashboard and the seats. I didn't even want to think about what Mom would do to us. I had my hands full with Helen, who was now hysterical. She threatened to break my rib cage if I didn't get her the hell out of there *right this instant.*

I floored it out of the parking lot and down a side street. The road was unlit and an eerie gust was stirring the newly fallen leaves. Mercifully, the tape recorder under the car seat had jammed. This was just fine by me, having now decided that I did not want to be memorialized in the school yearbook for having caused Helen Stockman to die in the front seat of my mom's station wagon. Helen was starting to calm down, although she was making some kind of gurgling noises and mumbling what sounded like, "Wait 'till I tell your mom about this. She's gonna kill you."

That's when Art's tape recorder decided to work.

Frankly, it even scared me. Art had throttled the tape deck up to full volume. "Hellll-en! Helllll-ennn! I want yoooouuu!" The suddenness of it caused me to swerve the car into someone's front yard. I do not know what happened next because Helen grabbed my hair with both fists and began shrieking, "Oh, God! Oh, God! David, let me out of here! I am going to throw up!"

The rest, as they say, was Halloween history. Helen did not throw up, although I am pretty certain her head spun all the way around. According to eyewitnesses, she whipped me mercilessly with one of her high heels for at least fifteen minutes, leaving a crater in my skull deep enough to hide a small pumpkin. Art pulled up behind us, fell out of his car, and rolled on the ground laughing so hard that his face was covered with drool.

Helen refused to go out with me ever again. She also told my mother the whole story. Mom told Art and me we should have our heads examined for doing such a mean thing. Mom was always telling us she was going to have our heads examined, but she never did it. Instead, she grounded us and made us spend an entire Saturday cleaning the station wagon. She made us pay for the gas, too.

The episode taught me a valuable lesson about pranks and having fun at someone else's expense. No matter what your brother tells you, it is impossible to remove ketchup stains from the dashboard of your mother's car.

Derby Day: The Agony of Victory

Every april thousands of moms and dads across America watch the calendar nervously as that infamous deadline creeps closer and closer. There is no way to escape the annual ritual that forces them to stay up late at night wrestling with complicated forms and instructions—pulling their hair because they have once again put it off until the last minute.

All you parents out there are nodding your heads

because you know what I'm talking about: the annual Pinewood Derby.

Pinewood Derby is a Cub Scout sporting event designed to demonstrate the patience and teamwork required to carve toy cars out of big chunks of wood and then race them in an organized competitive event. I break out in hives just thinking about it.

Until I became a Scout parent, I assumed that knowing how to handle power tools and carve objects out of raw wood was a natural skill that all young boys were born with—like knowing how to operate a DVD player or how to wait until the family is at a soccer game three miles from the nearest rest room before announcing that they can't hold it any longer. It turns out that if you hand a block of wood, some nails, and an electric drill to an eight-year-old boy, you do not end up with a character-building experience, or a racecar. You end up with a horrifying amount of damage to the garage walls.

Derby contestants usually start by buying an official Cub Scout Pinewood Derby Assembly Kit, which contains more rules and instructions than a federal tax return. You can also sign up for evening Pinewood Derby training classes and visit Web sites created by Derby veterans for Derby beginners (EXCLUSIVE SPEED SECRETS TO HELP YOU WIN EVERY RACE!! OUR VIDEOS SHOW YOU HOW!).

When you return home with your Derby supplies, it's a good idea to spread them out on the kitchen table and walk away. Go to bed and pray that the Pinewood Derby Fairy will visit your house during the night, remove your lump of raw pine, and leave a professionally carved, gleaming, screaming, racing machine. I did this and the Derby Fairy left my son a note that read: "You're in big trouble, kid. Woodworking is not your dad's strong suit. He once tried to install a simple clothes hook on the laundry room wall in your last house, and the people who live there now still invite friends over once a year to laugh at it."

As an alternative, tool-impaired parents can buy a pre-carved Pinewood Derby car at most hobby shops, which are easy to spot by the line of frantic Scout parents lined up at their doors every night during Derby season. There are many designs to pick from, including:

- **The Do-It-Yourselfer:** Just saw along the dotted lines. When it's done your kid will have a Derby car that resembles a doorstop with wheels but is less aerodynamically sound.
- **The Nightmare:** This car can be assembled quickly, after your young Cub Scout advises you for the first time that the Derby race is at 8:30 A.M. tomorrow.
- **The Professional:** This model is for supercompetitive

parents who insist that their kids excel in every organized activity, including nap time. It has a fuel-injected engine and front-wheel drive. It is also illegal and won't be allowed in the Derby.

After choosing a design, you and your child will enjoy several satisfying nanoseconds together painting and decorating his Derby entry. However, the instant you start explaining concepts like "priming the wood" and "not putting the cat's tail in the varnish" he will lose interest to the point that both of you will agree it would be best if he went outside to play and let you finish the car by yourself.

Then Derby Day arrives. At our school, the racetrack is assembled in the gymnasium, which is soon teeming with various character-building activities. Derby contestants are lubricating, sanding, and waxing—intensely focused on crafting a racecar that will kick the snot out of their opponents' cars. Those are the parents. The new Derby moms and dads are huddled around last year's winners, desperately groping for last-minute tips. ("You gotta bevel out the axle heads. Reduces downhill friction.")

As for the kids, they are at the other end of the gym keeping out of their parents' hair and playing something called Crash Basketball. It is similar to real basketball except that there are 345 players on each team and body tackling is apparently legal.

Thirty or forty minutes after the publicized start time, someone blows a whistle and the races begin. The gymnasium rocks with cheers and applause. The walls reverberate with the thrills of victory and the agonies of defeat.

"Yesss!" [Victorious mom punching a triumphant fist into the air.]

"Aw c--p!" [Losing dad, who forgot to bevel his axle heads.]

It's over in less than two hours. Tiny plastic trophies are presented to the winning Cubs, who immediately hand these to their parents and return to playing Crash Basketball. The moms start mopping the gym floor. The dads tear down the track, which is crated and stored in the boiler room, next to the volleyball equipment. Someone flicks off the lights.

As everyone heads to the parking lot, you see little boys hugging their parents and thanking them for all the hard work. Some of the Cubs are buzzing about next time. Next year, they say, they will have the fastest racecars of all.

Their parents nod. They know the next Pinewood Derby will be here before they know it. They can hardly wait.

Hey, Coach! Watch This Shot!

There is one sensitive issue that all parents in the Midwest dread facing as our children develop and become physically active.

No, it isn't sex. We are quite comfortable talking about sex with our kids, since most of them know more about it than we do.

FATHER: Honey, what, exactly, makes someone a "hottie"?

TEENAGER: This is, like, so *not* something I want to talk with you about.

FATHER: Thanks. I'm glad we had this talk.

The decision Heartland parents must face sooner or later is this: Do we want a tranquil, anxiety-free parenting experience, or do we want to coach our kid's youth basketball team?

Midwesterners are extremely serious about basketball. The game was invented here in 1891 by a minister-educator named James Naismith. Naismith wasn't really in the Midwest when he invented the game. He was in Massachusetts. But he moved to Kansas a few years later because that's where all the basketball fanatics were.

Thanks to Naismith, Midwest schoolchildren learn how

to dribble a ball between their legs before they learn the Ten Commandments. As you can imagine, this puts a lot of pressure on their parents, most of whom would rather volunteer to discuss sex with an entire gymnasium of teenagers than coach Little League hoops.

First-time parent-coaches discover immediately that they know even less about basketball than they do about sex. It surprises some of them to learn that there are two schools of thought about coaching in the Little Leagues. School 1 holds that the kids are supposed to have fun and that size and talent are not important. However, all the really athletic parents send their kids to School 2, which holds that School 1 is for wimps.

There also are two types of Little League basketball coaches. Coach Type A is the geeky Fred MacMurray type who knows nothing about the game but gives every kid equal game time regardless of the score. As a rookie coach you will never face one of these coaches.

All the teams you play will be coached by Type B. This is the highly competitive dad who played power forward in college. He requires his players to learn the North Carolina motion offense and the 1–3–1 trapping press defense. During the game he screams instructions like "Post up!" and "Set a pick!" and "Put a body on someone!" It is a waste of time to point out to him that these are third-graders.

Whether you want to or not, you will have to schedule weekly practice for your peewee hoopsters. This affords them a chance to work on critical game fundamentals such as dribbling between the legs, spinning a ball on the tip of the index finger, and launching three-point swish shots from half court. You also should keep a notepad to record each child's strengths and weaknesses. Like this:

- **Josh:** I have no idea . . .
- **Ricky:** Whatthehell?
- **Andrew:** OMIGODOMIGODOMIGOD

Upon arriving at the gym for your first game, try not to look at the opposing team warming up at the other end of the court. If you do, you may notice that they have expensive warm-up jumpsuits to match their uniforms, tattoos on their arms, a large repertoire of special plays—and even their smallest player can dunk. Instead, stay focused on getting through your first game without some parent calling you an idiot or screaming at you for not giving his child enough game time.

There is a teensy chance that things won't go well in your coaching debut. If so, signal for a "time-out" and call your players to the bench for an inspirational pep talk.

"Hey, you guys, you're doing great! They're only ahead 75–3, so let's slow it down a little. Jason, quit pinching Luke. Kyle, did you remind your parents that it was their turn to bring the pop?"

After the final buzzer jump up and say "Good game!" to everyone on the other team, including their coaches, assistant coaches, scouts, player agents, trainers, and publicists. Tell your players you are proud of their hustle and how they kept their shoes tied for most of the game. Also let the parents know how proud you are that hardly any of them screamed obscenities at you or the referees.

Then congratulate yourself. Thanks to you and James Naismith, these kids got to play in a real basketball game with real jerseys and real fans cheering for them. They had so much fun they can hardly wait for the next practice. Their one-armed half-court shots need a little work.

All in all, it could have been a lot worse. At least you didn't have to talk to them about sex.

To Whom It May Concern: Have a Merry Christmas

I have many good memories of Christmas in the Midwest. Hardly any of them involved snow. I hate that. What's the point of suffering through brutal Midwest summers if you don't at least get snow at Christmas? I think it snowed more when I was a kid, but hardly ever at Christmas. Sometimes it snowed after the holidays, which meant we didn't have to go to school. As far as I was concerned, that made up for Christmas.

I also remember opening presents around the Christmas tree with my family. My parents had seven kids, so opening gifts on Christmas morning usually took about five hours. It could have been done in half that time, but Mom insisted that every scrap of wrapping be stuffed into a trash bag as gifts were opened. This drove my brothers and me crazy. We wanted to open the presents quickly so we could go sledding. Until we remembered that it hadn't snowed.

One of our favorite holiday activities, however, was reading the end-of-the-year canned newsletters from old friends and relatives who had moved away but who still wanted us to know that they led interesting lives. The letters were full of happy news and achievements. Some were printed and folded like a miniature newspaper, with pictures and headlines (ANDREW WINS PRESCHOOL SCIENCE FAIR!!).

We still get these letters. Maybe you do, too. It remains a Christmas tradition in my house to read these out loud at dinner and laugh so hard the eggnog squirts out our noses.

Here's a sample:

To All Our Dear Friends Back Home,

Hello, to all our friends! We hope you don't mind this somewhat impersonal holiday greeting, but we just have so many friends we want to say hello to this time of year and our lives are so hectic we don't ever have time to stop and try to remember all your names.

This past year was a memorable one for our family. The highlight was moving into our new home at Executive Manor Plantation Creek Estate Gardens on-the-Green. We'd simply wanted a modest ranch so we'd have space to entertain our friends and sponsor occasional symphony concerts. But once we got started we just couldn't stop. Some who have visited so far tell us it reminds them of Bill Gates's new home outside Seattle. I think they're exaggerating a little. There are eleven bathrooms, nine bedrooms, a rooftop pool, a working volcano, and lots of room for *you* to come visit us.

Brandon graduated in May from Harvard Medical School. Not only did he finish second in his class, but he was also class valedictorian, and his professors say he's in line to be named U.S. surgeon general.

Our little princess, Tiffany, has one year left at the Rainey Brooke Debutante Country Club Academy for Girls. I don't know where she inherited all her brains, but she tells her father that she plans to get scholarship offers from even more New England colleges than he did! We are warmed by Tiff's passion to serve others. During the spring semester she chaired Rainey Brooke's "We Care" campaign to purchase rain canopies for the team benches on the girls' soccer field.

Roland—our baby!—turned thirteen in May. His favorite memory of the year is the two-month summer camp he attended in Minsk working as a translator for Russian humanitarian assistance programs. The coaches at Rainey Brooke Prep begged him to return as captain of the eighth-grade basketball team this year, but Rollie said he couldn't play sports and devote the necessary time to his fledgling import–export business. It was such a difficult decision for him, but we are so proud!

Are your lives as crazy as ours? Nathan's company had him traveling all over Europe this year. He loves being senior managing partner but says he hardly has time anymore for his favorite hobby—helicopter snow skiing in Aspen! In September Nathan got to ski with Al and Tipper Gore and they gave him two VIP tickets for a fund-raising gala starring Barbra Streisand. We wish all of you could have been there with us!

Somehow, Nathan also found time on the weekends this year to plant a half-acre rose garden for me. We hope you can come see it! My favorite part is the waterfall that runs from atop the

18-foot gazebo, across the Italianate marble terraced steps, and into a reflecting pool that the horses love to sip out of (see pictures enclosed).

The kids are after me to cut back my hectic schedule of civic activities. This year I co-chaired our Middleton Community Symphony's concert series. Over the July 4 holiday, we had Kathie Lee Gifford do an autograph signing. I don't know how we did it, but we raised $13,000 to hire a twenty-four-piece orchestra for Kathie Lee—she always insists on an orchestra for her guest appearances just in case someone asks her to sing something. Before she left she gave me a big hug and said she loved my hair.

I wish we had time to call each and every one of you and see how you are doing. But I know you understand. We hope you'll come visit us in the New Year. After all, we have lots of room! Have a great year, wherever you are!

The Richolsons—Marci, Nathan, Brandon, Tiffany, and Roland

Speaking of the Weather

Spring in the Heartland is a time for planting, basketball play-offs, bass fishing, Pinewood Derby, and pre-emergent crabgrass applications. It also is the time for severe storms. Twister season.

In the Tornado Belt it is impossible to avoid the weather. I don't mean avoiding the actual weather. You'd have to stay indoors all the time to do that, and then you'd never get that pre-emergent applied. What I mean is that you cannot avoid people who are constantly *talking about* the weather.

Midwesterners are fluent in meteorology. We speak weather. Day and night the radio and television stations drone about atmospheric conditions and dew points and air masses. The evening TV newscasts in my hometown devote more time to the weather than they do to basketball, if you can believe that. You cannot carry on a casual conversation at the grocery store checkout counter without a grasp of fundamental weather terms and expressions.

If you're planning a spring vacation in the Midwest, you should take the Doppler Radar Intelligence Quiz. It will test your command of the climate. It will definitely make it easier for you at the grocery store checkout lane.

My other advice is this: If you spot a funnel cloud, never try to outrun it and never crawl under a highway overpass. Trust me. I've lived here my whole life.

THE DOPPLER RADAR INTELLIGENCE QUIZ

1. Who is the exclusive source of "Doppler radar" emergency weather information?
   a. Fox 4 Storm Tracker Four-is-More Double Doppler Tower Cam.
   b. The Action News Live Power Digital Triple Doppler Oh Doo Dah Day Action News Storm Skycast.
   c. Kansas City Royals play-by-play announcer Denny Matthews.

2. Which of the following is not a real meteorological term?
   a. Inversion.
   b. Mucus.
   c. Dew point.
   d. Baccalaureate.

3. A very loud outdoor siren in your neighborhood means:
   a. Tornado warning.
   b. Tomato warning.
   c. Tax increase warning.

    d. The antitheft device on someone's BMW has
       malfunctioned again.

4. **If the National Weather Service announces that tornadoes are on the ground near you, it means:**
    a. Tornadoes are on the ground near you.
    b. You should go driving around with a video camera to see if tornadoes are really on the ground near you.
    c. It depends on what they mean by "on the ground."

5. **Write an essay of 1,000 words or less explaining the difference between a "tornado watch" and a "tornado warning." Use additional paper if necessary.**
ANSWER: This is one of those unsolved scientific mysteries. We suppose it has never occurred to the National Weather Service to simply flash messages on the TV that say, "Tornadoes Are Near Your House" or, "Some Tornadoes Are Seriously Considering Touching Down Near Your House."

6. **While driving in a rainstorm, you approach an intersection so inundated by floodwater that the tops of telephone poles can barely be seen protruding from the surface. You should:**
   a. Put the pedal to the floor and race straight ahead, yelling, "Yahooo!"
   b. Wait until it's apparent that seven other cars have been sucked under the water. Then, after looking both ways, carefully determine that just because those cars didn't make it, there's no reason why yours won't.

7. **If your house is located on one of those flood-plains that get flooded every single year, it is perfectly reasonable for you to:**
   a. Refuse to move out of the floodplain and demand that taxpayers repair your home after each flood.
   b. Act totally surprised when a television reporter asks you if you've ever heard about flood insurance.

8. **After a severe storm, your piles of fallen tree limbs should be:**
   a. Dragged out to the street and shot with a rifle.
   b. Neatly folded, placed in a No. 10 envelope, and

mailed to the mayor's office at city hall. Warning: Post office will not deliver without postage.

c. Piled helter-skelter at the curb in a humongous tangle the size of Indonesia that will block the sidewalks and create dangerous blind spots for motorists.

9. **Which of the following is not recognized by the National Weather Service as an official hail size?**
   a. Softball sized.
   b. Zucchini sized.
   c. Labrador retriever sized.

10. **If you are on the golf course when golf-ball-sizc hail begins to fall, what should you do?**
    a. Play the one closest to the tee.
    b. Keep your head down on your follow-through.
    c. Take cover in the clubhouse and order a Double Doppler on the rocks.

11. **If you notice lightning bolts striking the ground all around you, you should:**
    a. Put down the beer and climb down slowly off the John Deere.

  b. Stand in a doorway.

  c. Kiss someone who is standing in a doorway.

12. What, technically, is an "air mass"?

  a. A bunch of air up in the sky.

  b. A religious service held on airplanes.

  c. There is no such thing. We're pretty sure there also is no such thing as a "dew point."

13. Where do clouds come from?

  a. They are emitted from the back of high-flying aircraft, which is why meteorologists refer to them as "jet streams."

  b. Seattle.

14. Where do weather forecasters go for fun?

ANSWER: We can't imagine. However, if you rearrange the letters in *meteorologist* it spells *to motel orgies*. But this is only a theory.

15. Which of the following explains the phenomenon of underground cable television lines being disrupted during weather no more severe than a sudden breeze?

  a. It cannot be explained by modern science.

b. It is caused by interference from Doppler radar.

c. This occurs so homeowners will quit watching television and go outdoors and check the weather for themselves.

SIX

IN EVERY FAMILY

Making Wishes

I've always been an uneasy parent.

It worried me that I was supposed to know, from the outset, how to be a role model for children. Where was I supposed to have learned this? In high school? From *Family Circle*? Every day as a parent feels like on-the-job training without the training.

I could swear my parents were never this uneasy. After they got over the initial shock of no new Glenn Miller recordings, Arthur and Christianne slid into the cockpit of parenthood like fighter pilots who had trained for it all their lives. They flipped the switches of their lives, and ours, as though they had written the operating manual on raising children.

My generation isn't so at ease. We are like the neurotic gardener who creates breathtaking flower beds but sees only the weeds. Our kids begin life with more advantages and opportunities than kids of any other era, and still we cannot relax. All the livelong day we are filled with dread that our children won't grow up happy and it'll be all *our* fault. It'll be our fault because we tried to hold down two careers and two car payments and way too many civic activities. Our kids will hate us because we pushed them into Little League soccer too soon or computer classes too late.

We dig up one anxiety and two more pop up in its place, like spring dandelions. We wish someone would just tell us that everything will be okay and that our kids will turn out fine.

I explained this theory recently to my mom. She laughed and said I needed my head examined.

"You've got to be kidding."

About what?

"About your father and me not being worried."

If you were, it didn't show.

"You were a child," she said. "What did you know about worry?"

What did you worry about?

She rolled her eyes. "About everything. When you were born, Steve was only four and Annette was two. If we went anywhere, Dad held Steve and I held Annette. Then we had you and we thought, *Now what do we do? Who's going to hold David?*"

You must have figured it out.

"You always figure it out," she said. "But you never stop worrying about your children."

Does worrying work?

Mom pulled her reading glasses down to her nose and

looked me at across the top of the frames. "You turned out okay, didn't you?"

I'm still an uneasy parent, but I don't feel bad about it anymore. I think my mother was right. Parents live with anxiety every day and we survive it. And our children survive having us as parents.

We make mistakes because we never read the child-raising manuals and we only paid attention to half the things our own parents told us. Our kids know this, which is why they are only paying attention to half of what we tell them. They are not keeping score and they are not expecting miracles. Our kids know they are lucky to have someone who has so many wishes and dreams for them, and so many worries. If this were not so, then the children would be the uneasy ones.

Our kids may not turn out as we wished, but a part of us will always be a part of them. They, too, will become uneasy one day, just like their parents and their parents before them. Like us they will make big wishes for their children and dream big dreams. In the spring they will dig dandelions that grow faster than they can pluck them.

Like us they will learn that your parents may stop holding you and feeding you and teaching you how to behave.

But they can never stop worrying about you. You wouldn't want it any other way.

Making Lists

When I was little, I wrote Santa every year telling him what I wanted for Christmas. On my list every year was a drum set. Santa brought many of the things I asked for, but he never brought the drum set. If I ever see him again, I plan to ask about this.

My brothers and sisters and I always left milk and cookies by the fireplace on Christmas Eve, for Santa and the reindeer. The next morning, we found an empty glass, a pile of crumbs, and a "thank you" from a Santa in handwriting that looked a lot like my father's. This was probably just a coincidence.

On Christmas morning it felt good to know that Santa had been in our home, that he had eaten our cookies, and that he had read our letters, even if we didn't get everything we wanted. Santa seemed like a good listener, someone you could talk to. So when I had my own child, I decided to stay in touch with the big guy.

On my son Max's fifth Christmas Eve, we left snacks by the fireplace. There were no milk or cookies in the house, so we improvised.

Max made his wish list and showed it to me. There were a few surprises. I told him I'm sure Santa would do his best, then I put him to bed. I went back downstairs to the fireplace and wrote my own letter.

I told Santa I was the kid who'd asked for the drum set all those years ago, but that I wasn't sore about it anymore. I told him I was a parent now and I understood that sometimes you don't get everything you ask for. Sometimes you get things you didn't ask for.

Now that I have a child of my own, I told him, I have a whole new Christmas list.

DEAR SANTA:

My five-year-old boy scribbled out his Christmas list. It's there by the fireplace. The Coke and M&M's are from him, in case you're hungry. You know five-year-olds these days. The Cheez-Its are from me.

Santa, if you don't mind, I thought I'd go ahead and leave my list, too. It's long, but do what you can.

It's all I want for Christmas.

Santa, let my little boy grow up still believing that he has the funniest dad in the neighborhood.

Give him many close friends, both boys and girls. May

they fill his days with adventure, security and dirty finger-nails.

Leave his mom and me some magic dust that will keep him just the size he is now. We'd just as soon he stayed five years old and three feet, four inches.

If he must grow up, make sure he still wants to sit on my lap at bedtime and read The *Frog and the Toad*.

If you can help it, Santa, never let him be sent into war. His mother and I love our country, but we love our five-year-old boy more.

While you're at it, give our world leaders a copy of *The Killer Angels,* Michael Shaara's retelling of the Battle of Gettysburg. May it remind them that too many moms and dads have wept at Christmas for soldiers who died in battles that needn't have been fought.

<hr>

Let our house always be filled with slamming doors and toilet seats, which are the official sounds of little boys.

Break it to him gently, Santa, that his dad won't always be able to carry him to bed at night or brush his teeth for him. Teach him courage in the face of such change.

Let him understand that no matter how nice you are to everyone, the world will sometimes break your heart. As you know, Santa, a child's feelings are fragile as moth wings.

Let him become a piano player, a soccer star, or a priest. Or all three. Anything but a tax-and-spend politician.

Give him a hunger for books, music, and geography. May he be the first kid in kindergarten to be able to find Madagascar on a map.

The kid's a born artist, Santa, so send more crayons. May our kitchen window and refrigerator doors be ever plastered with his sketches of surreal rainbows and horses with big ears.

Through the years steer him oh-so-carefully to that little girl destined to be his bride. Let his mother and me still be around when he walks her down the aisle. If there is a just God, her daddy will be obscenely rich.

Grant him a heart that will cherish what his parents did right and forgive us for the mistakes we surely will have made over a lifetime of raising him.

Let him not hold it against us that he was born with my chin and his mother's ears. Time will teach him that these are God's ways of girding him for life's adversities.

Hold him steady on the day that he learns the truth about you and the Easter Bunny. May he take the news better than I did.

While you're flying around the heavens, Santa, make sure God has heard our prayer for this child: Lead my little boy not into temptation; deliver him from evil.

Be careful out there, Santa. And close the flue on your way up.

Forgiveness

USA Today ran a cover story in December 2002 about happiness. Along with its typical charts and graphs and everything, it posed the question, "Why are some people happy and others not?"

The story quoted University of Michigan psychologist Christopher Peterson as saying that, based on his research, the trait most strongly linked to happiness is forgiveness.

"It's the queen of all virtues, and probably the hardest to come by," he said.

I sent Peterson an e-mail and asked if I could talk to him about this. He e-mailed back and told me there was nothing more to say. His research uncovered the correlation. He added that I could check the data for myself if I wanted. Happy, serene people, he said, are people who forgive easily. In turn, they are drawn to those who forgive them.

I didn't check Peterson's research. I believe him. There is nothing more to say.

It was nearly 2:00 A.M. and I was not supposed to be sitting here in the car in the driveway of my parents' house. I was supposed to be inside, in my bed, asleep.

I brought my mom's station wagon to a halt and left the engine running. I left the car door ajar so it wouldn't make any noise when I got back in, then I lifted the garage door as slowly. The door made a groaning racket as it retracted into the ceiling, and I cursed it.

I got back into the driver's seat without shutting the door. The car rolled forward into the garage. I killed the engine and flicked off the headlights.

So far so good. The whole night had been good. I still hadn't gotten the nerve to kiss Helen Stockman yet, but this made two dates in one week. I must be doing something right. The only mistake was losing track of the time. It was July 1970, the summer after my junior year of high school, and I knew better. I knew I should have called from Helen's house hours ago, to let someone know where I was.

I stayed in the driver's seat a few moments to wait for silence. Mom's blue Pontiac station wagon was a colossal gas guzzler that made all kinds of engine pinging and knocking sounds after you shut it off. In the dark stillness of my parent's garage at 2:00 A.M., the pings and knocks sounded thunderous. I cursed them, too.

Slowly, without breathing, I reached for the door handle. As I did, my eyes glanced upward into the rearview mirror.

⸺⸺

There was a man standing in the garage, right behind the car.

He didn't say a word, even after I stepped out of the car. For a second I felt a chill of fear like a cold wind. Then I noticed a trail of cigar smoke rising up in front of his face. Both thick, hairy arms were stuffed into the pockets of baggy pants that seemed one size too short and two sizes too loose. He was silhouetted against the light of a street lamp, but I could see that he wore a threadbare, torn T-shirt with paint blotches down the front.

I would know that silhouette anywhere. My father wore those same clothes every night after work. He even wore the torn tee shirt to bed.

"Come inside," he said. I could tell this was not going to be good. "Leave the garage door open and come inside."

I walked into the living room, which was just inside the front door. My mother was already there, sitting at the end of the couch right next to the reading lamp. Another silhouette. So far, I hadn't seen any eyes, ears, or mouths.

Dad followed me in, and he sat down behind a desk at the other end of the room. To talk to them this way I had to turn my head one direction to see Dad and the other way to see Mom. This was not going to be good.

"Do you know what time it is?" Mom asked.

Parents always open with that question. I do it now with my own son. I guess I am secretly hoping that he will look at his watch and exclaim, "Holy cow! No way! It can't be 2:00 A.M.! Is it 2:00 A.M.? My watch must be broken. I had no idea . . ." Mom didn't wait for an answer.

"Do you know what has been going through our minds?"

I do, I said.

"No, you do not," she said.

Her voice quivered and her eyes were wet. "Only when you have children of your own will you know how frightened we were. We didn't know if you were alive or dead in the street somewhere. We didn't even know who to call."

Then it was Dad's turn. "When you're the parent, you can do what you want. We are the parents here and you go by our rules."

No argument from me. My eyes were starting to adjust. I could see their faces. I had seen it before. It's the look on a parent's face as he reaches for a child who has suddenly darted into a busy street without looking. The breathing stops. The eyes bulge. The expression is a mixture of panic, anger, and relief. Even in the dim light, I could see all these things on the faces of my parents. They were only now beginning to exhale.

Dad drew on his cigar. "Only your family will worry about you like this, David. You must think about us."

Then he asked me what I had to say for myself.

———✳———

"I'm sorry," I said.

It must have been the right answer. Dad stood up. He poked the cigar back in his mouth and used both hands to hike up his baggy pants.

"You can go to bed now. First, give your mother a hug. You scared the dickens out of her. She's been sitting over there praying the rosary all night."

I hugged Mom and she hugged back. Dad preferred handshakes, which was fine with me.

Dad said he was going outside to close the garage door, so I headed upstairs to my room. I looked back down the stairs and I could see Mom was still sitting on the end of the couch by the lamp, rosary beads in hand.

If they had stopped worrying, I couldn't tell. They would never stop worrying. They were parents. But they had stopped being angry. If someone asks me many years from now what I remember most about my mom and dad, I will say that they were never very good at staying angry.

I undressed and slid into bed. My parents never said another word about that night again.

Before You Go:
I'm Glad You Were My Mom

"No man is poor who has a godly mother."
— Abraham Lincoln

I am fifty years old but I still hear a voice inside my head saying, "Don't go out in the cold with wet hair" and, "Look people in the eye when you talk to them," and "Tuck your shirt in."

I'd know that voice anywhere. My mother repeated herself a lot, saying the same thing over and over again, often in the same breath. As she did this, she poked you with her elbow. You didn't have to agree with her, but you were going to hear her. My mom believed in using her voice and her elbow. She believed that people should stand up for themselves and speak their minds.

Sometimes after a funeral she would say, to whoever was

within poking distance, "All those nice things people say about you when you die. Hell's bells, they ought to tell you those things while you're still alive."

My mother said "hell's bells" a lot. I had no idea what this meant or why there would be bells in hell. Maybe they ring them to remind us to say nice things about other people before it's too late.

I told my mom she was right. I told her that one of these days I was going to tell everyone all the things I plan to say about her on the day we lay her to rest. So here it goes.

They say my mother is gone, but that's not really true.

I can see her whenever I want. All I have to do is close my eyes and there she is. I can see her tossing her head back and laughing louder than everyone else at some funny thing I said or wrote. I can hear her clapping longer than anyone else when one of us kids sang a song at school or caught a pop fly on the baseball diamond.

No room was the same after Chris Chartrand entered it, or after she left. Long after our childhoods, my brothers and sisters and I were flabbergasted at how often some old family acquaintance would pick us out of a crowd. Then we figured it out. They remembered us because they had never forgotten our mother.

Christianne Hauber had always turned heads. The fifth child of German Catholic Midwest immigrants, she was accustomed to being the center of attention. Her family and friends called her Tuddy. ("Like *tootsie*," she explained, "but rhymes with *goody*.") As a little girl she was a fetching tomboy with loose limbs and a feisty spirit. As a young woman she was a short stemmed American rose with a Katharine Hepburn allure. Tuddy the little girl liked hunting butterflies with her brothers, ice skating, and snow sledding. Chris the woman liked singing around a piano, dancing, and parties. She also liked strong, shy men.

Art Chartrand was so shy that, on their first date, he wouldn't even come to her house to pick her up. Instead, she met him at the PlayMore, a popular Midwest ice rink with a dance hall on the second floor.

"He was so shy it was pitiful," Chris said. "I had to take his arm and put it around my waist." By evening's end Art had found his nerve. "He kissed me good night, and that was it. He was so polite and gentle. I knew it was over then. I knew what I wanted."

Chris Chartrand had always wanted to be a nurse, but now she wanted Art, too. So when nursing school was over for her and World War II was over for him, Chris had to choose between career and family. As with many women of her generation, it was an easy decision. Besides, being a wife and mother felt just like being a nurse. She could love and nurture and take care of others who needed her. Chris Chartrand knew she was good at that. She could do that forever.

My mother was like the Midwest weather. She blew hot and cold, one extreme to another. When she was happy, she was hysterically happy. I wrote a poem in second grade called "I Think Mice Are Nice," and she called all our relatives to read it to them. "See?" she was still telling people at my fortieth birthday party. "He was a writer even back then."

When she was sad, she was inconsolable. I can still see her kneeling next to the bed the night my brother Ed died at twenty-two. She knelt there all evening, crying and praying at the top of her voice. I was as dumbstruck then at the vastness of her grief as I am now, as a parent, at the boundlessness of her faith. God had taken her child and God would heal her. When He did it again, years later, Chris Chartrand was back on her knees. I think she was so good at praying that God told her things He doesn't tell everyone. I think He let her know why bad things must happen to good people.

God may have eased the miseries of my mother's heart, but when it came to her body, He was less compassionate. As she grew older, she cursed the bones and joints that made it painful to garden or cook or do other things she was good at. Her arthritic back and fingers were naughty children who disobeyed and ignored her. You had to live in our house to understand that my mother could tolerate anything except being ignored.

<hr />

There is a hole in my life now where my mother used to be. I fill it sometimes by leafing through the leather-bound family photo albums that she maintained as meticulously and lovingly as the rows of geraniums in clay pots that lined our cement patio. Squeezing the pages between my fingers, I am overcome by the sense that I am stirring the embers of her life, feeling the warmth of her spirit one more time. In every photo she is smiling and radiantly beautiful, just as I will always remember her.

Much of what I have become I trace to my father. Like him I am methodical, predictable, a little too shy. The rest of me is my mother. I cry too easily and I repeat myself a lot. And, like my brothers and sisters, I am mulishly stubborn. We can't help it; we were born that way. If some salesperson or clerk told my mom, "We can't do that," she would reply, "Why not?" Then she'd stand there until she got what she wanted. She knew what she wanted and she usually got it.

There's more I could tell you about my mother, stuff that would make you laugh until we both cried. Which is precisely the problem. It's hard to write stuff like this when you can hardly see the keyboard.

⸻

"You'll probably tell everyone someday what a nutty mother you had," she said. She said this many times. Then she poked me with her elbow.

"Hell's bells, tell them anything you want. But for crying out loud, tell them I raised you to stand up for yourself."

I told them, Mom. I told them everything. I told them how nutty you were and how you taught us about family and photo albums and faith and standing up for ourselves. I told them how glad I was that you were my mother. Most of all, I'm glad I told you. I wanted you to be the first to know.

Only Your Family

I'm all for telling people you love them, especially while they are alive to hear it. This is especially true with children. Preachers and talk-show hosts are always telling us we don't talk enough to our kids.

But what if talking doesn't help? What if talking makes things worse?

I'm a good parent but a lousy speaker. I get jumpy talking to my wife about sex, let alone talking to my son about it. Writing, however, forces me to organize my thoughts. On the typed page the sentences possess a rhythm and flow. On my lips they tumble out like scattered marbles. I think I'm making extremely good sense but I notice my son staring back at me the way you look at someone who is having a nervous breakdown.

Before telephones and computers lovers and loved ones depended on letters. Today hardly anyone sends letters or receives them. Children e-mail and double-click their way into Internet chat rooms. They send "Instant Messages" that receive instant replies, both of which require as much forethought as instant coffee. In an instant the message and the thought have vanished without a trace.

Now and then, however, I lose my appetite for instant food and instant talk. I am in the mood for nutritious communication with my son, something that requires more time and ingredients but leaves a better aftertaste. So I write to him.

I write about nothing important, just those everyday things you want to say to your child—just in case you don't get another chance.

Dear Max,

Your mom and I don't say this often enough, but you are the sunshine of our lives. You make us laugh. You make us proud. We know how lucky we are.

This stuff we are supposed to talk to our kids about is too tricky to be left to improvisational chatter. Sure, face-to-face communication is a good idea. But it leaves an awful lot to chance. For one thing, you might screw it up. The phone rings. Then the yellow Labrador starts eating the kitchen rug. It's hard to focus; the messages come tumbling and tripping over each other like loose mice. Mice are nice, but writing is better.

Sometimes, Max, your mom and I lie awake at night wishing we could go in your bedroom and pick you up like we did when you were a baby and hold you and protect you from all the heartache in the world. Isn't that silly?

Writing letters helps me sort it out ahead of time. There are no blurted words that I wish later on hadn't been said. In a letter I can say everything I wanted to say, the way I want to say it. My son hears what I wanted him to hear.

We know we are on tough on you sometimes, Max. We want to make sure you don't chase after the wrong things. Sometimes people chase something all their lives and then, after they've caught it, they are sad to find out it wasn't what they wanted after all. On the other hand, when you find what makes you happy, go for it.

A letter lets a parent compete with all the other signals being gathered by a kid's radar. The difficult decisions in life don't involve right against wrong, but right against right. Anyone can explain to a child the differences between choosing to be a YMCA coach or an ax murderer. Helping him process all the other options isn't so easy.

Every day our kids are listening to friends and celebrities whose viewpoints don't square with what we have taught them. The messages they get from the media and the movies are carefully scripted, market-tested, and rehearsed. Up against all that, I'd rather not wing it. I want to write it down and get it right the first time.

You know what makes for a happy life, Max? It isn't money or a great job. It is love. The richest people in the world aren't happy unless they come home every night to someone they can hardly wait to see, someone who fills their days with love. Pennilessness isn't the worst thing that can happen to you, my son. It's loneliness.

I'm all for talking to children. Talking takes less time, but I have nothing more important to do. A letter leaves a clear message and an imperishable paper trail—something my son can fold close to his chest and read over and over again long after I'm gone.

That's all your mom and I wanted to say, Max. We hope you didn't mind us writing it out like this. We're not very good talkers. We're only your parents. We would have said these things in person to you, but we knew we'd never get through it without crying. And the dog just ate the kitchen rug.

We love you very much.
—Mom and Dad

Dear Graduate:
Remember Who You Are

If I were a good speaker I would give a high school commencement address.

I have no idea why a high school would want me as its commencement speaker, unless perhaps Tom Brokaw or Jay Leno had to cancel at the last minute. I would do it for half the fee, however.

My speech wouldn't be very funny or informative. I would tell students going off to college what their parents would tell them. The assembled graduates would probably roll their eyes and sigh. They would whisper to one another how they had already heard this all before. But I would make them hear it again.

> Most of you are no doubt agog over the adventures that await you as you leave home soon for college. Like being able to eat pizza every day for breakfast. I am not here to titillate you with such fancies.
>
> You will discover soon enough the thorny choices that are the bedmates of personal freedom. What I wish to alert you to are the sights and sounds that *won't* be there when you are left on campus to fend for yourselves.

You'll know right off that this isn't high school any-more when you wake up and realize there is no one telling you:

To get out of bed.

To get back in bed.

To turn off the television.

To avoid strangers.

To go to bed and *I swear I am not kidding this time.*

To quit picking your nose.

To wipe your nose.

But not on your sleeve.

To help with the dishes.

To comb your hair, cut it, or get it out of your eyes.

To make your bed.

To stand up straight.

To speak up.

To clean the "pigsty" in your room.

To come here *right now* before I count to three.

To look at your mother when she talks to you.

To *not* look at your mother that way.

To eat your dinner.

To take out the trash.

To settle down.

To grow up.

To stop growing up so fast.

To get in the bathtub.

To get out of the bathtub.

To *walk*.

To hurry up.

To check your shoes for mud.

To go ask your father.

To dress warm.

To say thank you.

To say you're sorry.

To look both ways.

To wipe your hands.

But not on your clean shirt.

To kiss your mother good-bye.

Because *I said so*.

See what you're going to miss?

You're going to miss having teachers who know everyone in your family, who shop and worship in your neighborhood. Believe me, to the university professors you'll be just another face. You'll have to siphon from the well of their knowledge, because they will not force you to drink from it.

Never again will anyone remind you to do your homework on a Sunday night. You can party all weekend. It's your life. Waste it only if you dare.

You are about to jump into the deep end of the pool

of life, to sink or swim on your own. Let no one throw you in too soon. There is no shame in waiting. If you aren't ready for this much responsibility and independence, then take some time off first. Read and travel. College will still be there when you get back—when you'll be more equipped to take what life dishes out.

Campus life will not so much build your character as reveal it. Brace yourself now for the relativism you will find on campus. Professors and dorm buddies will suggest to you that the rights and wrongs you learned at home are just circumstantial grays, that to reach a moral conclusion is to impose it on them. Stick to your guns. These people are not your friends.

Watch out for religious cults that prey on frightened and lonely college freshmen. There's no harm sharing your prayers and dreams with them, but when they demand your mind and your possessions, it's time to walk away.

If you must choose between what Mom and Dad told you is right and wrong and what your college philosophy professor tells you, my money is with Mom and Dad. They have a bigger investment in you.

One last thing: Be not surprised by the tears streaking your parents' faces this fall as they drop you off at the dormitory. They are not sad. They weep because they are having a hallucinogenic experience. All they know is that yesterday you were frogs and snails and puppy dogs' tails, sugar and spice and all things nice. They have no earthly idea when you turned into this cocky young adult. It is a surreal, mind-altering experience that will be much clearer to you when your own kids leave for college.

You, too, will cry now and then as you realize how much your family means to you and how well they prepared you for this moment. Remember always who you are; stand up for what you have become.

But for crying out loud, stand up *straight*.

Before I count to three.

What Child Is This

It is 7:00 A.M. and there is someone in my little boy's bed.

Pushing up through the blanket is the outline of a man's body. Draped over the bedside are a man's hands. There are sneakers on the floor, but they are too large to be my little boy's.

This is his room. I should know. I come here every morning to wake him for school.

"Time to get up, bud!" I always announce, as I tug the blanket from his face. He calls it his "blankie." He tugs back and asks to sleep for five more minutes. I always say okay. We do this two or three times.

Slowly, a little boy stirs to life. Soft feet land on a soft carpet. Lights are flicked on. A toilet flushes and a toilet seat crashes against porcelain. Doors slam. I hear the sniffing of a runny nose.

But now something is different. I do not hear little-boy noises. I hear an electric shaver and coughing—a deep, masculine cough. Coat hangers rattle and last night's college basketball scores blare from a TV turned up a little too loud. Tall, handsome young men make these sounds, not little boys.

Although there is no little boy in the room, there are little boy things. LEGO spaceships and Teenage Mutant Ninja Turtle action figures still stand sentry atop the bookshelves. League basketball team photos and Cub Scout Pinewood Derby trophies stand watch along the walls. Maybe they are waiting for the little boy to return. Maybe they are trying to prevent him from leaving. But it's too late.

Not only is my little boy gone, but now this young man is leaving, too. He is heading to college. The Ninja Turtle toys and the basketball photos will stay behind. So will his mother and I. That's what worries me the most.

I will have to pass by here every morning at 7:00 A.M. and see this room and all the little-boy things. I will have to look in and wonder.

I will wonder if someone else is waking him the way I did. I will wonder if he is already out of bed or if he has rolled over and pulled his blankie to his chin.

If it's a cold, dark morning, perhaps he will imagine that he hears my footsteps in the room and the sound of my voice telling him to go back to sleep. The most glorious sounds a child can hear, or a parent can make, are the words: "No school today. It snowed." I wonder how hard it will be now to listen to the radio on snowy winter mornings and hear the school-closing reports and not be able to wake my little boy so I can tell him to go back to sleep. I wonder how many times this room will break my heart.

This room is where our house began to stir every morning. This is where our days began. It was more than a major fact; it was the only fact. So I will pass this room every morning and wonder why it ended so soon, and what happened to my little boy

In the meantime I will wake this man who is sleeping in my son's bed. I will tell him I love him, even though I have no idea who he is or how he got here. I will pull the blankie up to his chin and try not to think about tomorrow.

Then I will tell him he can go back to sleep. For five more minutes.

For Sale, by Owner

It was time to sell the family house. Thanks to the inheritance left by his late brother, Arthur finally had the money to buy something smaller, a house with fewer leaves to rake, fewer gutters to clean, fewer walls to paint, and fewer stairs to climb.

Two of the children were dead and the other five had long since moved out. Arthur and Christianne had no use anymore for such a big house. It was full of memories and photo albums, but they planned to take those things with them.

It wasn't easy putting out the FOR SALE sign. The front yard with its hard, clay soil fought back against the sign's metal prongs, as though someone were driving a stake into its heart. Arthur planted the sign but he could not bring himself to write the "for sale" listing for the newspaper. He asked me to do it.

"I don't know what to say or where to begin," I told my father.

"Something will come to you," Arthur said. "You're a writer. Just write what you know."

So I wrote what I knew. It felt as though someone had driven a stake into my heart.

FOR SALE: Split-level wood-frame house on large, treed lot. Has been home to loud, wacky Chartrand family for thirty-five years. Kids are grown and gone. Family no longer able to keep it up; can barely stand to let it go.

ALMOST NOTHING NEW! If you want new, sleek, and shiny, look somewhere else!

QUAINT PENNSYLVANIA DUTCH DESIGN! Looks like a place Ward and June Cleaver might have owned. All windowsills well maintained by father of seven who gave up his weekends to paint and mow and repair when he could have been doing something else if he'd wanted to. He didn't want to. Baseboards and cabinets kept meticulously clean by strong-willed German mother who is absolved from all guilt for the fact that some of her children turned out to be complete slobs.

WALLS IN GOOD CONDITION. If they talk, ask about time in 1969 that teenage son was exploring in attic and rammed foot through insulation floor that also happened to be living room ceiling. We laughed until we wet ourselves.

HARDWOOD FLOORS EVERYWHERE! We think! Never seen them. Every inch of floor has been covered with carpet for decades. If you had four boys and three girls dragging roller skates and Tonka trucks across your floors all day, you'd cover them with carpet, too. The floors, we mean.

SMALL BATHROOMS! That's the way they built them in those days before people decided they needed bathrooms and bedrooms the size of Wisconsin. Owners somehow managed to get seven children bathed, pottied, and off to school every day without double sinks, Jacuzzi tubs, and private bathrooms for every child. In these rooms everything is within reach!

CLOSETS are tiny and cramped by today's standards—but cavernous when nine years old and crammed inside with four friends during hide-and-seek games. *Note:* Still looking for mint-condition 1961 Roger Maris card last seen behind vacuum cleaner in entry closet, or possibly buried in backyard near swing set.

SPECIAL FEATURE: Cool, first-floor laundry chute that, for some reason, drops dirty laundry 50 feet from washing machine.

NO HEARTH ROOM! None of today's pretentious design features. No cathedral ceilings or game rooms or wraparound cedar decks. Den level has tiny wet bar with refrigerator. Fridge stays with house; we couldn't get it out. Sellers' children always assumed that owning two refrigerators made them the richest, luckiest family in the world.

SOME WALL TREATMENTS TO REMAIN! This includes faded 1967 *Mad Magazine* sticker on wood paneling in den that says THIS STICKER WAS NOT HERE YESTERDAY. Many scratches, gouges, pockmarks on walls that once were covered with family photos. Buyer should bring lots of new photos, or spackling paste.

FORMAL DINING ROOM! Site of 362 birthday parties, thirty-five Thanksgiving and Christmas dinners, a couple of dozen First Communions and nearly forty wedding anniversaries. Dining room also doubles as temporary storage for school science fair projects and enough buckets of Halloween candy to serve 300 to 400 trick-or-treaters.

EAT-IN KITCHEN! Nothing like today's kitchens! Not spacious! No cooking islands or designer pantries! A good venue for family Monopoly games, however, or staying up until midnight doing homework. Built-in intercom/radio system somewhere under wallpaper.

EXTERIOR WOOD LAP SIDING in great shape, thanks to many summers of painting supervised by father who insisted that every inch of old paint first be melted off with handheld propane torches. You can hardly see the spot anymore where west side of house was temporarily set ablaze by torch-wielding son who eventually went on to a writing career that thankfully does not involve handling live flames.

LARGE BACKYARD! Perfect for touch football. Has been the scene of 246 croquet games and 357 Home Run Derby tournaments where anything hit onto a rain gutter was an automatic triple. Many trees, bushes, and flower beds make this the perfect yard for hiding Easter eggs! Owners still haven't found many of them! Side yards feature lots of dirt with big rocks that can be lifted to reveal interesting worms and slugs.

TWO-CAR GARAGE—hardly ever used! Never had room for cars. Has only been used to store bicycles, toys, garden equipment, pet supplies, lawn mowers, clay flower pots, home repair projects, paint cans, ladders, and folding tables for lemonade stands.

GOOD, STRONG FOUNDATION! If it held up this family, it'll hold yours. Dry basement. Lately, however, some tears seen streaking the walls. Pay no attention. House may be worried. Doubts it will ever have it so good again.

ASKING PRICE: House will go to buyer with best offer. The memories stay with us.

For the Record

While working on this book, I asked Dad to jot down some dates and details about his banking career.

A few weeks later he stepped into my office. "Here, I made this for you." He handed me a standard audiotape cassette. "I hope I did it right."

Instead of writing his career memoirs, Dad had dictated them into an old tape recorder. He said he found it in his garage, with the original AAs in the battery compartment. The handwriting on the cassette indicated it had originally been used to tape a news program off the radio, about twenty years ago.

"I just taped over what was on there," he said. "I hope it's okay."

❊✕❊

Dad was never comfortable around electronic equipment. He could repair cars, fix toilets, and unclog drains, but computers, answering machines, and VCRs made him uneasy. While dictating into the recorder, he stopped every ten minutes to convince himself that the machine was actually recording his voice.

"I'm gonna stop here now and see if this thing is working," he says ten or twelve times on the tape. The recording stops. Then there is a click and his voice returns. "Well, I guess it's working so I'll just keep going."

Go too fast and you'll make mistakes. Always check your work. Do it right the first time. The epitaph for Arthur Chartrand's life.

Driving home from the airport one evening, I pop the cassette into the tape player on my Camry. Most of it is an impromptu but strikingly well-organized recitation of Dad's early years in banking. It's exactly what I need for my book.

Then the tape stops. A few seconds later there is a click and silence. Then his voice returns. He has something else to say.

"Your mother and I were very fortunate," he says.

Fortunate? Just about every unfair, painful thing that can happen to two good people happened to this man and woman. Now he gets a chance to leave some final thoughts and he's telling me how fortunate they were?

"All the things that happened and the way everyone closed ranks with us," he says.

"The way everyone has stayed together. That's what

kept us going. And I forgot to mention your mother. There is always one strong person and she's been it. She was the pillar of strength that kept you kids going. She kept me going."

I can hear the sound of his lips smacking apart, and his tongue clicking in the back of his throat. Dad made those mouth sounds when he was having trouble speaking, which wasn't very often.

"It's all wrapped up in family and children. That's your life. And now I really am going to end up now."

There is a click and the recording stops. My father didn't say another word.

LAST WRITES

Many times I have considered how I'd like to spend my last day, assuming God lets me know ahead of time which day is my last.

The thought of porking out on Cheez-Its and Peanut M&M's appeals greatly to me. It also might be nice to have a morning when I don't have to floss my teeth.

The evening, however, would be spent partying with my family. We will dance to Sam Cooke and The Drifters and drink chardonnay from paper cups until we are all tipsy. Scattered around the floor will be the old family scrapbooks and videotapes that catalog my life, the achievements and the screwups. We will spend hours trying to assemble them, like the dots in those draw-by-number children's books, the ones where you don't know what the picture looks like until you connect the last dot.

"All finished," some tipsy sister or cousin will say, staring down at the sprawl of dots and memories. "What does it look like? What do you see?"

From where we are standing, it won't be much of a picture: just an ordinary life spent doing the same dull and random things that people everywhere do every day. From a distance that's all you can see. It's like looking down at the Midwest from an airplane window.

So I will ask everyone to sit on the floor with me and take a closer look. I will remind them to be careful not to spill their wine, though I'm not sure why. After today, the carpet stains will be someone else's problem.

One by one, we will examine the pieces of the picture. I will point out that the memories may seem ordinary and commonplace, but they had been unpredictable and full of surprise. The arc of my life had been altered, over and over, by events I could never have foreseen. What steadied me each time was the healing, loving power of family and friends. It is something you cannot not see in pictures or from a distance, but it was there all along. It was there before me and will be there after I am gone.

The Cheez-Its depleted and my face aglow from the chardonnay, I will ask everyone to come closer so I can feel that power one last time. We will hug and weep, as family and friends do at times like these. Then I'll make my final request, something that can be asked only of those who have loved you the most, who have shared your darkest nights and your brightest days. I'll ask someone to run out and buy more Cheez-Its.

About the Author

David Chartrand is an award-winning syndicated newspaper columnist who writes humor and commentary from his home in Olathe, Kansas. You can e-mail him by visiting his Web site at www.david chartrand.com, or you can write David c/o Reader Response/Editorial Department, The Globe Pequot Press, 246 Goose Lane, P.O. Box 480, Guilford, CT 06437.